MW01515691

# The Good Shepherd

A Guide to Understanding and Connecting with God-inspired Leadership

*Adebayo Ayorinde*

# The Good Shepherd

A Guide to Understanding and Connecting
with God-inspired Leadership

*Adebayo Ayorinde*

**Hebron Publishers**

**The Good Shepherd** (*A Guide to Understanding and Connecting with God-inspired Leadership*)

*by* **Adebayo Ayorinde**

© **2021 Hebron Publishers,** 3 Egbema Close, Borikiri, Port-Harcourt, NIGERIA

*Unless otherwise indicated, all Scripture quotations in this book are from the King James Version (KJV) of the Holy Bible. Other versions of the Bible cited in this book are CEV (Contemporary English Version), NLT (New Living Translation), MSG (The Message Bible), and NCV(New Century Version)*

**All rights reserved.** No part of this book may be reproduced, stored in a retrieval system or transmitted in any form or by any means, electronic, mechanical, photocopying, recording or otherwise without the prior permission of the publisher or in accordance with the provisions of the Copyright, Designs and Patents Act 1988 or under the terms of any licence permitting limited copying issued by the Copyright Licensing Agency.

**ISBN: 979-871-5408-22-8**

**Cover photo:** Biegun Wschodni (https://unsplash.com/@ biegunwschodni)

**Cover Design:** Hebron Publishers

# DEDICATION

*This book is dedicated to*

## *God Almighty*

# FOREWORD

The twenty-third Psalm is the most renown Psalm in the Bible. Reading it gives comfort to the heart of the reader that there is indeed the provision, preservation, and protection of God, the Good Shepherd. In this book, Adebayo Ayorinde has taken David's Shepherd in Psalm 23 and linked Him with the Good Shepherd described by the Lord Jesus Christ in the tenth chapter of John's gospel. In marrying both portions of Scripture, Adebayo gives us a depth of understanding of leadership and followership in the Christian experience using the relationship between the shepherd and his sheep. Nothing helps our understanding better than real-life examples. In this book, there are several such testimonies.

*"The Good Shepherd"* is a book that challenges Christians to trust and follow Jesus, not just as their Saviour and Lord, but more importantly, as their Leader who desires the best for them. Adebayo challenges Christians to develop their knowledge of the Good Shepherd and their ability to hear Him. If people do not know who they are following, they will misunderstand or completely ignore whatever good thing he is trying to do for them. Thus, Adebayo challenges Christians to know the Lord Jesus Christ in an intimate relationship and learn to hear from Him daily. He enumerates ways and means of hearing from God along with real-life testimonies of their application. Without question, if we are not hearing from God, we cannot even follow Him!

Perhaps the most profound and, I dare say, audacious part of this book is Adebayo's proposition of "The Good Shepherd Leadership Model" (TGSLM) and its application to secular leadership by Christians. He challenges Christians to live like their Leader, the Good Shepherd, and apply His leadership approach to everyday living. One fascinating aspect of his TGSLM views leadership as "a caring mother" rather than "a bossy boss."

His TGSLM requires a shift from the paradigm of the traditional corporate leadership models that focus more on production—output—to a leadership model that focuses on the products' producers. Of course, for the conventional corporate leaders, the question will be, "How do we measure productivity?" but Adebayo's TGSLM is about developing people who will do anything for the leader because they know that the leader has their backs! An organization's productivity using TGSLM will be the individuals' wealth and well-being as the basis for determining the organization's overall productivity. This new leadership paradigm proposed by Adebayo can be applied in the home, neighbourhood, public sector, private sector, government, and organizations, but only by saved and sanctified individuals patterned in the mould of Jesus.

The conclusion in this book, should trigger prayer by all discerning Christians for effective leadership, nurturing, and caring of their charges. I pray that as you read through this book and arrive at the 'Final Words', you would have gained much to make you a better Christian modelled in the pattern of the Good Shepherd, the Lord Jesus Christ, and His way of life and leadership.

*Abraham Raymond Eli*

# PREFACE

While teaching on the subject *"From Sheep Coats to The Palace"*, I spoke about the Good Shepherd in passing, but God impressed it upon my spirit to teach further on it. Considering that this fresh leading was about a subject that would take more than a one-day sermon, I broke it into a series of teachings that spanned several weeks, all of which have formed the core material for this book. By God's anointing and Spirit, I pray that you too will connect with the life and fire that burned through this teaching so that you can connect with the more profound truth of the mysteries of God's ways, as entrenched in this offering.

The truth about humanity today is that many people navigate the sea of life without a compass. As a result, they lose their way because the challenges and circumstances they face often toss them into unfamiliar terrains. People are open to dangers of all kinds and unfortunate eventualities, just as a rudderless ship or sheep without a shepherd. Instead of finding the Creator's compass, people seek help from all the wrong places, get into more trouble, and stray farther away from God.

King Solomon captured the situation perfectly when he observed that,

> *"God made man simple, but man has made his life complicated"* (***Ecclesiastes 7:29 CEV***)

Today, you do not have to look hard or far before seeing the effects of these complications all around. The first impression you get whenever you encounter the media is a glaring picture of how bad things have become. It is the picture of a sick world—of wars, terror, political upheavals, economic crises, strange diseases, natural disasters, and heightened godlessness manifested through unprecedented levels of immorality!

Those conversant with Scripture know that these are only a manifestation of what the scriptures have foretold. They are pointers to the fact that we are living in a time where there is gross failing in virtually every aspect of human experience, including family life, personal or business relationships, politics, and religion. Value systems have crumbled, moral foundations are broken, 'crazy' has gradually become the new 'normal', and sorrow multiplies across the nations!

Sadly, these trends will continue because as humankind's ways become more at variance with God's Master plan for a meaningful and healthy existence (as laid out in the Holy Book), so will the challenges of this life. The patriarch Job said,

> *"Man that is born of a woman is of a few days and full of trouble." (**Job 14:1**)*

Today, the days seem fewer and the troubles more. While humanity struggles to find answers, the one question that many fail to ask is, "How did we get here?" The answer lies in the fact that human beings, by default, are born with the power of choice into a world where their destiny is ultimately decided by whose leadership they subscribe to—God's or Satan's.

There you have it—it has been a leadership problem all along! Our struggles and failings come down to the issue of leadership: who is leading you, and whose leadership playbook are you applying in all that you do?

This teaching offers a leadership template for humankind as mirrored by Christ's parable of *"The Good Shepherd"*. The 23rd chapter of the Psalms, along with Jesus' timeless allegory in the 10th chapter of John's gospel, provides an excellent connection that illuminates the core elements of God's character which every believer in Christ, and indeed, every sincere leader—either in the spiritual or secular world—should possess.

In the end, *The Good Shepherd* provides an infallible compass for navigating through life and understanding how to align with God's purpose.

Come with me and let us explore the scriptures and contemporary testimonies that will enable you to understand what is involved in living a God-led life, and more importantly, God's leadership model for today's Christian.

# ACKNOWLEDGEMENTS

L ife is about people. One way or the other, 'people' will always be at the heart of everything we do, either as the target audience or those who make things happen. Against this backdrop, I am deeply grateful to the Redeemed Christian Church of God's hierarchy, under the humble leadership of Daddy G.O, Pastor E. A. Adeboye, for the opportunity to serve in the ministry. I am equally grateful to the entire membership of Light House Parish, Lekki, Lagos—this book would probably not have seen the light of day if there were no flock to serve. In particular, my heartfelt gratitude goes to the pastorate and workers, my co-labourers in the Lord's vineyard.

The book you have in your hand, which started from scribbled notes in my study to a series of teachings at the church, would not have materialized without the input of those who make things happen professionally. In this regard, I thank Godspower Michael-Eyakwaire, Team Lead at Mindworks Media, for his role in birthing this project. I remember telling him that he was God-sent at the point of engagement for work on the manuscript. In the end, he left me with no doubts whatsoever. Thank you for seamlessly becoming an extension of my thinking through ideas that were critical in shaping the content.

I am equally grateful to Shedrach Maisamari of the Light House Parish, Lekki, who edited and reviewed the manuscript for his excellent work. Your candid observations and professional touch have helped in shaping this work into a better offering.

Finally, to my wife, Yemisi Ayorinde, there will never be enough words to thank you for the fantastic support you give in all I do. Combining ministry and professional work can be very demanding, with constant international travel pressures and meeting up with church programmes taking their toll on work-life balance. But through it all, your understanding remains a priceless gift. Thank you so much!

# CONTENTS

# INTRODUCTION

# THE BRIDGE BETWEEN DAVID'S PSALM AND CHRIST'S PARABLE

The Bible is replete with stories of God's dealings with humanity, especially the sample nation of Israel, Abraham's seed. From Genesis to Revelation, we see the picture of a God who desires to have fellowship with His creation. God reveals Himself as the One who will go to any length to protect, provide for, and deliver His people. We also see a God who will not compromise His standards and, as such, will reprimand His loved ones just as much as He would go to any length to defend them. So perfect are His ways and mighty His power that His people always have faith in His ability to deliver them in times of trouble.

Perhaps, no other person in the entire Bible could capture the essence of this faithfulness, as did David when he penned down the twenty-third chapter of the Psalms. Possibly, because of his own shepherd boy experience growing up, David, in those lines, poured out what has become one of the greatest expressions of trust in God by anybody, living or dead. When David said,

> *"The Lord is my shepherd,"*

he revelled in the blessings he was enjoying as a result. David spoke about the two-way connection between the shepherd and the sheep. That connection is what the shepherd does for the sheep and what the sheep do to enjoy the shepherd.

So rock-solid is the level of assurance displayed by David in this Psalm that it has become one of the most recited portions of Scripture or benediction in Christendom today, and indeed, around the world at large. I can bet that you repeat the sixth verse of this Psalm regularly:

> *"Surely goodness and mercy shall follow me all the days of my life: and I will dwell in the house of the LORD for ever."*
> *(Psalm 23:6)*

Unfortunately, many people today do not understand what should drive that level of faith in God and trust in Him. And because they do not know Him enough, when they make that declaration, regardless of how many times they recite this verse, it does not awaken corresponding faith in them. When push turns to shove, and life's waters become turbulent, they still get to run everywhere looking for help because they do not know the Good Shepherd as David did.

# THE VITALITY OF KNOWING GOD AT THE DAVID LEVEL

Do you remember the story of the seven sons of Sceva in **Acts 19:14-17**? The demon said to them: "Paul, I know; Jesus, I know; who are you to be boasting of God like them?" He *knew* that these men did not *know* God at *the David level*! That is why you cannot appropriate the authority of what you do not have a connection with, no matter how loud your confession!

When you are unplugged from God, the adversary knows, and He will use it against you.

As a true child of God who desires to live a victorious Christian life, you must know God as David did—as *the Good Shepherd*—to command the kind of relationship portrayed in **Psalm 23**. And Jesus came to make our relationship with God meaningful and eternal. In **John 17:3**, Jesus said,

> *"And this is life eternal, that they might know thee, the only true God, and Jesus Christ, whom thou hast sent."*

The knowledge of God is the starting point in the journey of transformation. To discern and follow the right leadership in a cacophony of voices—in the spiritual and physical realms—we must comprehensively grasp this subject. Jesus gave a parable that serves as a bridge to knowing God as David did—as *the Good Shepherd*. As you read on, you will begin to understand the representation of God's character as the Good Shepherd by David in **Psalm 23** and by Jesus in **John 10:1-18**.

These scripture passages are a perfect template for building and boosting your faith in God and developing a leadership model that does not fail. I pray that at the end of the day, the Holy Spirit will transform your life in the name of Jesus Christ. Therefore, before we proceed further, I would love for you to pray this prayer: "Father, in this journey of life, let me not go astray in the name of Jesus Christ."

*You cannot appropriate the authority of what you do not have a connection with, no matter how loud your confession!*

Now, let us examine the subject of godly leadership.

# PART ONE

## *Understanding The Good Shepherd*

# TABLE OF CONTENTS FOR PART ONE

# Chapter 1

The Good Shepherd

# Christ, The Good Shepherd

*His forever, only His:*

*Who the Lord and me shall part?*

*Ah, with what a rest of bliss*

*Christ can fill the loving heart.*

*Heaven and earth may fade and flee,*

*Firstborn light in gloom decline;*

*But, while God and I shall be,*

*I am His, and He is mine*

*The first stanza of the Hymn, "Loved with Everlasting Love" (1876)*

*by George Wade Robinson, 1838-1877*

In **Genesis 3:1-13**, we see how Adam and Eve fell because they followed—listened to—the devil. God created Adam and Eve and placed them in the Garden of Eden, along with a set of instructions to follow. The foundation of their relationship with God was God's leadership. Sadly, the devil, through the serpent, appeared on the scene and beguiled Eve, when he asked,

> *"Did God really say you must not eat any of the fruit in the garden?" (**Genesis 3:1, NLT**)*

Eve's response and the serpent's subsequent remarks created doubt in her about God, and from that moment on, she, and by her prodding, her husband, Adam, unwittingly subscribed to the leadership of another—the devil! From then on, Adam and Eve, as representing all of humankind, went astray, following Satan's direction!

Once Adam and Eve went astray, God came looking for them, but they went into hiding. And God called out to Adam,

> *"Where are you?" (**Genesis 3:9, NLT**)*

and he responded,

> *"I heard you, so I hid. I was afraid because I was naked." (**Genesis 3:10, NLT**)*

to which God said,

> *"Who told you that you were naked?..." (**Genesis 3:11, NLT**)*

What God was saying was, "I am your Creator. I am the one leading you. And now you are telling Me that you are naked? Who told you that? I certainly did not tell you that!" and Adam stuttered, giving untenable excuses.

And that was how humankind fell—because their progenitors followed someone else; Satan. In giving heed to Satan's counsel, Adam and Eve, and the whole of humanity, came under Satan's leadership and control. But that was not the end of humanity—there was hope, and it was in

Jesus Christ!

Now, to **John 10:1-18**:

> *"Verily, verily, I say unto you, He that entereth not by the door into the sheepfold, but climbeth up some other way, the same is a thief and a robber. ²But he that entereth in by the door is the shepherd of the sheep. ³To him the porter openeth; and the sheep hear his voice: and he calleth his own sheep by name, and leadeth them out. ⁴And when he putteth forth his own sheep, he goeth before them, and the sheep follow him: for they know his voice. ⁵And a stranger will they not follow, but will flee from him: for they know not the voice of strangers. ⁶This parable spake Jesus unto them: but they understood not what things they were which he spake unto them. ⁷Then said Jesus unto them again, verily, verily, I say unto you, I am the door of the sheep. ⁸All that ever came before me are thieves and robbers: but the sheep did not hear them. ⁹I am the door: by me if any man enter in, he shall be saved, and shall go in and out, and find pasture. ¹⁰The thief cometh not, but for to steal, and to kill, and to destroy: I am come that they might have life, and that they might have it more abundantly. ¹¹I am the good shepherd: the good shepherd giveth his life for the sheep. ¹²But he that is an hireling, and not the shepherd, whose own the sheep are not, seeth the wolf coming, and leaveth the sheep, and fleeth: and the wolf catcheth them, and scattereth the sheep. ¹³The hireling fleeth, because he is an hireling, and careth not for the sheep. ¹⁴I am the good shepherd, and know my sheep, and am known of mine. ¹⁵As the Father knoweth me, even so know I the Father: and I lay down my life for the sheep. ¹⁶And other sheep I have, which are not of this fold: them also I must bring, and they shall hear my voice; and there shall be one fold, and one shepherd. ¹⁷Therefore doth my Father love me, because I lay down my life, that I might take it again. ¹⁸No man taketh it from me, but I lay it down of myself. I have power to lay it down, and I have power to take it again. This commandment have I received of my Father."*

Not understanding what Jesus was saying in this scripture passage is catastrophic to the Christian. Jesus spoke about hirelings and thieves. He said,

*"The thief cometh not but for to steal, kill and destroy...."*

He wants you to understand that if you follow a thief, the ultimate goal of that thief is to destroy you! Forget about what you see now, it might appear to be something nice, but it is only an illusion. The end of it will be an unmitigated disaster. That is why you need to understand what the Lord is saying in this parable.

In this book, we shall explore Jesus' parable in two parts, namely;

(a) The Characteristics of the Good Shepherd;
(b) The Characteristics of the Sheep.

Jesus points out three key characteristics which summarize the personality of the Good Shepherd, and these are:

1. He leads His sheep.
2. He cares for His sheep.
3. He knows His sheep.

He also states the traits which the sheep display:

1. They follow the Shepherd,
2. They know the Shepherd,
3. They know the voice of the Shepherd, and
4. They trust the Shepherd.

*If you follow a thief, the end of it will be an unmitigated disaster.*

The sum of the sheep's characteristics is that they will not follow anyone except the Shepherd and, therefore, cannot be deceived. We shall dig deeper into this in Part Two of this book. For now, it is pertinent that we get to know the Good Shepherd in the context of what He does for the sheep.

# Chapter 2

**The Good Shepherd**

# The Good Shepherd Leads His Sheep

*He leadeth me: O blessed thought!*
*O words with heavenly comfort fraught!*
*Whate'er I do, where'er I be,*
*still 'tis God's hand that leadeth me.*

*He leadeth me, he leadeth me;*
*by his own hand he leadeth me:*
*his faithful follower I would be,*
*for by his hand he leadeth me.*

*The first stanza and refrain of "He leadeth me"*
*(1862)*

*by Joseph Gilmore, 1834-1918*

T he first of the Good Shepherd's characteristic is that *He leads the sheep*. And that brings us to the question: What does it take to lead? We will attempt to answer this question using the template of the Good Shepherd.

# CORE ESSENTIALS OF CHRIST'S LEADERSHIP QUALITIES

We shall be looking at the essentials of Jesus' leadership qualities that make Him the leader and essential guide of the sheep.

### 1. HE KNOWS THE TERRAIN

If you must lead, then *you must know the terrain*.

Whenever I travel to the United States of America and drive, the first thing I do is plug in the GPS (Global Positioning System) to find my way around while driving. This I do because I am not familiar with the terrain. But once the GPS is on, it helps me navigate through the complex road networks, and it leads me precisely every inch of the way to my desired destination. Knowing the lay of the land is what leadership entails: whoever will lead must know the terrain!

*Christianity is not a religion but a way of life, bringing man into a one-on-one relationship with his Creator, and is the solution to sin.*

The good news is, God created the earth and everything therein and thus knows the 'lay of the land' and how to navigate life!

**Isaiah 40:28** says,

> *"Hast thou not known? Hast thou not heard, that the everlasting God, the LORD, the Creator of the ends of the earth, fainteth not, neither is weary? There is no searching of his understanding."*

and **Psalm 24:1** affirms that:

> *"The earth is the LORD'S, and the fullness thereof; the world, and they that dwell therein."*

It follows that if anyone must lead the people who inhabit the earth, it must be the Creator Himself!

## 2. HE KNOWS THE WAY

We can also derive from the Good Shepherd's example that if someone must lead, it should be the person who *knows the way!*

In **John 14:6**, Jesus said,

> *"I am the way, the truth, and the life: no man cometh unto the Father, but by me."*

Therefore, if Jesus is the Way, why would you follow anyone else? But if you choose to follow someone else, then I do not believe that you sincerely desire to get to your destination because Jesus is the Way!

Christianity is not a religion but a way of life. It brings man into a one-on-one relationship with his Creator. It is the solution to sin—no other "religion" can proffer a solution for sin.

Some would say that He was a fictional figure in the Bible, yet the Adversary, the devil, is severally recorded in the Bible as testifying of Him to be the Son of God. Why would the devil testify of Jesus if He is not real?

Think about it; there is no other religion where the devil testifies of any prophet. What we have are people testifying of those prophets or sages. But when it gets to a point where the devil himself says,

> *"What have we to do with thee, Jesus, thou Son of God? art thou come hither to torment us before the time?" (Matthew 8:29)*

You must understand that this witness is quite different from so many other things we may have been hearing.

Jesus is the Way! If you must lead, then you need to know 'the Way.' If you must lead, you must have access to light; else, you will be walking in pitch darkness; you cannot see where you are going.

---

*"Then spake Jesus again unto them, saying, I am the light
of the world: he that followeth me shall not walk in darkness, but shall have the light of life." (**John 8:12**)*

We can vividly see Christ's leadership supremacy—He is the Way, the
Creator, and the Light! Therefore, if anyone should lead you, He is best
qualified!

Also important is ***the all-knowing dimension*** of the Good Shepherd's
character. It implies that if you must lead, then you must be 'all-knowing' to know every consequence of your actions.

For example, if you have to decide between two job offers, how would
you go about that? It can be confusing to make the right choice. Ordinarily, being human, if one job offered one hundred thousand, and the
other would pay one hundred and twenty thousand, the obvious choice
would be the job that pays twenty thousand more. But do you know
whether the better paying job would end after six months? You would
have to consult with someone wiser than yourself—someone who does
not operate by sight! The Bible speaks of the wisdom of God, thus:

*the foolishness of God is wiser than men; and the weakness
of God is stronger than men. (**1 Corinthians 1:25**)*

So, even if God were to be 'foolish' (no disrespect intended!) He is still
wiser than the wisest man on earth! Of course, we know that God is
Wisdom Personified!

Ordinarily, one cannot possibly ignore a higher paying job for a lesser
paying one without following God's leading. If you have to decide on
one option out of numerous possibilities, you will need to follow Jesus's
leading and get it right.

Therefore, the 'all-knowing' requirement of one who must lead, de-
mands that the leader predict the outcome of every step they are taking
with accuracy. In other words, they should be able to predict the result
of their actions or decisions accurately. They should ask, for example:
"If I invest in such and such a business; what would be the outcome?"
Naturally, human beings cannot know such things. However, Jesus
knows. That is why He says of Himself,

*"I am Alpha and Omega, the beginning and the ending,*

*saith the Lord, which is, and which was, and which is to come, the Almighty." (**Revelation 1:8**)*

Therefore, before you even commence any venture, He already knows the end! How amazing! The question then is: **Why do people not ask the One who knows the end from the beginning before they start anything?**

*If you must lead, you must be 'all-knowing' to know every consequence of your actions.*

My submission is that Jesus is more than qualified to lead you. There is no point following after another.

# REASONS WHY THE LORD JESUS IS BEST QUALIFIED TO LEAD YOU

I present below my strong reasons from Scripture why the Lord Jesus is best qualified to lead you in any endeavour whatsoever in life.

### 1. JESUS KNOWS THE WAY OF ETERNAL LIFE — THE WAY OF SALVATION

There are many things that you and I do not know. In **Matthew 7:14**, the Bible says,

> *"Because strait is the gate, and narrow is the way, which leadeth unto life, and **few there be that find it**."*

Note the emphasis on the words, *'few there be that find it.'*

Now, if only a few people can find the way of eternal life and salvation, that tells us that it is possible to miss the way! Many people have followed others, and they have gone astray. And many more are still following them as you read this. If you are looking for the way to eternal life, the hard truth is that *the narrow way* is the way; and to get unto that path, you had better follow Jesus. Moses understood the importance of this. That is why when Israel sinned, he stood before God on behalf of the people and prayed thus:

> *"Yet now, if thou wilt forgive their sin—; and if not, blot*

*me, I pray thee, out of thy book which thou hast written."*
*(Exodus 32:32)*

Now, that was a very dangerous prayer. God had told Moses, "Look, they are a stiffed-necked people—they can go on their own. I do not need to go before them anymore." Still, Moses went to God in intercession and said, "You cannot abandon these people now." (**Exodus 33:1-16**). What an intercessor! That was the intercession that got God to again lead Israel in the wilderness.

In the course of that intense intercession, Moses had told God: "If You do not go with us, then blot my name out of Your Book which You have written." The seriousness of that! I pray that the Holy Ghost will explain it to you.

If you are not born again, please understand that there is a Book that God has written. If there were no such Book, Moses would not have talked about *the book*. You need to understand that your name is inscribed in that book; if not, he would have said *erase* my name. Instead, Moses said, *blot*, meaning that a conscious effort is required to remove it. Friend, you must ensure that your name is in that *book*. You can do that right now by saying this prayer: "Lord Jesus, I acknowledge your sacrifice on the cross for me. I realise I was born a sinner. I confess all my sins and repent of them this moment. I accept you into my heart as my personal Lord and Saviour from this day forward. Amen."

Congratulations! If you said that with sincerity in your heart, your name is now in *the book*!

**2. JESUS KNOWS THE WAY OF PROSPERITY AND ABUNDANCE**

When you look at **Luke 5:1-11**, many Christians today are like Peter—a super fisherman who knew everything about his trade. But it happened that the same guy came out and fished all day but caught nothing. I am sure if you were to have asked Peter, he would have said something like: "There is nothing I don't know about fishing. I know where the fish stay in the water, and I know the time to catch them!" Just like you and your business: Do you know everything about your business? Are you a super engineer or doctor? Are you a great tactician in everything you do, like Peter? Yet, the Bible says the man caught nothing! Maybe you have not been successful either?

When Jesus came on the scene, He said to Peter, "You have been fishing in shallow water!" He then told Peter it was time to launch into the deep. You may want to ask, "Why was the veteran fishing in shallow waters?" I will tell you straight up: it is because the risk associated with shallow waters is minimal. But much more than that, even when you think you would get more fish in deep waters, you are also likely to risk losing your life. That is why Someone had better be leading you. So, Jesus said to Peter, "Now, this is the place to launch", and the Bible records that the man caught a multitude of fishes when he followed Jesus' leading.

*"The earth is the Lord's and the fullness thereof!"* (**Psalm 24:1**)

*To ensure that your name is in that book, you must repent of sin by saying this prayer: "Lord Jesus, I acknowledge your sacrifice on the cross for me. I realise I was born a sinner. I confess all my sins and repent of them this moment. I accept you into my heart as my personal Lord and Saviour from this day forward. Amen."*

You just have to let that sink in at all times.

You may have been chasing after some money-making venture, but in truth, you do not know where the money is. Silver and gold belong to God (**Haggai 2:8**), and He owns the cattle upon a thousand hills (**Psalm 50:10**). If you are "working like an elephant but eating like an ant", as the saying goes, chances are you are not following Jesus.

A friend of mine once shared a testimony with me. At a particular time in his life, he used to get up every day looking for business for his company. Then one day, God said to him, "Don't leave your house again. Stop roaming around from one office to another." So, he decided to wait on the Lord for direction. He stayed at home for about three weeks, at which point, he said to himself, "Is this not a sure road to poverty?" Just then, God told him to go and buy two heavy-duty pumps. He acted accordingly and bought two heavy-duty pumps.

After this time, he waited for about four months for contracts to lease out the pump, but none surfaced. Then finally, God said to him, "Leave Port Harcourt (Nigeria) and go to Ghana". So, he made a move to Ghana. On getting there, my friend asked God, "Where do I go?" and God told him to stay in his hotel. So, he stayed put in the hotel where he lodged. After about three days of sleeping and waking in the hotel, he went to an office where he did not know anyone by the Holy Spirit's leading. When he got there, he requested to see the Managing Director. The secretary opened a door and directed his attention to a man on the phone, indicating that he was the Managing Director. So, he gave his business card to the secretary to give to the Managing Director.

As the secretary handed the card to the Managing Director, he immediately ended the call and requested my friend to come into his office. Once he was in the office, he asked him if he had pumps! The Managing Director described the specifications of the two pumps that my friend had bought some months earlier. He even went on to lament about how he had been calling everywhere to find those particular pumps, and nobody had been able to deliver them. My friend responded that he had them, and right there, the Managing Director gave him an initial one-year contract, and after just about three months into the agreement, my friend paid for the pumps in full!

And that is how Jesus, the Good Shepherd, can lead you into prosperity—when you follow the One who owns the silver and gold, and you stop running around town, catching nothing! I pray that God will help you embrace this level of revelation, in the name of Jesus. Recall the Bible story about the lepers at the gates of Samaria in **2 Kings 7:3-8?** Their condition meant that they were rejected, but God led them to abundance, just the way He would lead you also into your abundance when you follow Him.

### 3. A CRUCIAL LESSON FROM GERAR

In Isaac's life, there once was a famine in the land where he lived, and Isaac got up, ready to run away, but the Lord said, "No, stay in Gerar, do not go anywhere!" And the Bible said Isaac sowed during the famine, and in that same year, he reaped a hundred-fold! You see, what many people do not understand is this: if God is leading you, you can still have some issues here and there, but once you are sure it is God, beloved, you can be confident that He can never be wrong!

God told Isaac, "Stay in Gerar", and guess what followed? The Bible says Isaac dug the first well, and the natives of that land strove with him. They fought him and told him to get out of there!" Yet God had asked Isaac to stay in that land! He dug the second well, and they fought with him over that too. But by the time he dug the third well, Isaac got to his Rehoboth, for God had made room for him! (**Genesis 26:1-33**)

## 4. FROM ISAAC'S WELLS TO THE OIL FIELDS OF ALASKA

Let us switch from ancient times to more recent history. If you drill your first oil well in the oil business, and it is dry, and you leave to drill a second well, and you again leave because it is dry, rest assured that another company will come and find that oil and reap where you had started. The example of what happened in the oil fields of Alaska is instructive here.

One of the most significant oil fields in the world, located in Alaska, was sold by one company to another because the selling company did not see much potential to retain the oil field. Their geologists had reasoned, "There is nothing here." It turned out that the oil field was a goldmine for the new company that acquired it!

It is pertinent to state that being led or getting it right with oil prospecting is such a big deal in the oil sector. For a company to want to let go of an oil well, they must have tried various profitability assessments—you are looking at the highest level of risk mitigation and Return on Investment (ROI) assessments. The operational processes involved usually get more capital intensive and complicated as you progress from dry land to swampy areas, shallow waters, and ultimately, deep-sea or offshore operations. In a world like that, being led by God is priceless!

*God's leading is not necessarily issue-free; it requires that you completely depend on His guidance to pull through.*

Just as in the case of Isaac, if God sends you somewhere, you better stay there. The point here is that you cannot go wrong with God leading you.

For example, Jesus knows the right spouse for you. You are taking too much of a risk and selling yourself short because you are eager to live forever with someone. You may be making the wrong decision because your choice will be sentimental—looks, economic status, etc. Unless God leads you, you will err! On your own, you will end up with troubles you cannot begin to imagine, and you will be locked up in that trouble for the rest of your life! So, the big question is: "Why do you not ask the Lord?"

In **Genesis 24**, Abraham sent his servant to get a wife for his son, Isaac. As he embarked on the assignment, the servant prayed to God and asked that He be granted good speed, thus:

> *"O LORD God of my master Abraham, I pray thee, send*
> *me good speed this day, and shew kindness unto my mas-*
> *ter Abraham. [13]Behold, I stand here by the well of water;*
> *and the daughters of the men of the city come out to draw*
> *water: [14]And let it come to pass, that the damsel to whom*
> *I shall say, Let down thy pitcher, I pray thee, that I may*
> *drink; and she shall say, Drink, and I will give thy camels*
> *drink also: let the same be she that thou hast appointed for*
> *thy servant Isaac; and thereby shall I know that thou hast*
> *shewed kindness unto my master." [15]And it came to pass,*
> *before he had done speaking, that, behold, Rebekah came out,*
> *who was born to Bethuel, son of Milcah, the wife of Nahor,*
> *Abraham's brother, with her pitcher upon her shoulder."*
> *(**Genesis 24:12-15**)*

At the snap of the finger, the Lord granted him Godspeed! If you trust God for a spouse, as you are reading this book, the Lord will give you good speed; your husband or wife is coming your way speedily.

From this Bible account, when Abraham's eldest servant finally brought Rebecca to Isaac, the Bible says, when Isaac saw Rebecca, he fell in love with her instantly! Things got complicated because most people cannot deal with or understand why Rebecca was barren. If Rebecca, the One God chose for Isaac, was barren, maybe God was a liar? Far from it, but that is God for you! He says that His ways are not our ways (**Isaiah 58:5**). His ways are past finding out (**Romans 11:3**).

Like Isaac, who got a great wife through God's leading but had to contend with her being barren, some people today are in the right places because God led them there, but because they have issues, they begin to cry, "No, no, no, this cannot be God's leading!" But as I pointed out before in Isaac's experience in Gerar, what you must understand is that God's leading does not necessarily have to be issue-free; it requires that you depend on His guidance to pull through.

That is why the sheep trusts the Shepherd because they know that the Shepherd gave His life for them. I sincerely hope you can get this: if a Man gives His life for you, what else can He not give you?

*"He that spared not his own Son, but delivered him up for us all, how shall he not with him also freely give us all things?" ( Romans 8:32)*

Jesus will never lead you astray! He knows the right spouse, the right job, the suitable investment, the right move for you. He knows everything!

Many of God's people today are making investments without God; they are operating by sight. Everybody is running, and you are just running along! Now, this is the problem with many people today; they are walking by sight. I pray God to elevate you out of that level in the name of Jesus Christ.

Look at the story of David: He got to a location where they had taken his wife and his whole family. The natural thing to do in that circumstance would be to run after the captors immediately. But David did not do that. Instead, he sought the face of God in prayers asking, "God, should I follow them?" Even when it was his right, David was still asking for permission! Is it not his right to pursue after the captors and rescue his wife and children? Yet, he asked for God's direction. Today, many are fighting over things for which they should ask God first, and because they did not ask, they get into trouble. In David's case, he asked God first, "Should I pursue? Will I overtake? Would I recover all?" And God said to him, "Pursue, overtake, and you will recover all." (**1 Samuel 30:1-18**)

Jesus knows the way out of your trouble! He led Peter out of prison! In **Acts 12:1-11**, we read how King Herod killed James, John's brother, and then arrested Peter and kept him locked up. Afterwards, an angel of the Lord showed up and took Peter out of prison. I pray that everyone reading this book who is in any form of unjust imprisonment will be taken out today in the name of Jesus Christ. An end has come to your imprisonment in the name of Jesus! Today is your day of freedom!

# GOD'S ZOMBIE BLUEPRINT

I pray that you become God's 'zombie' by the time you finish reading this book. I am speaking of being entirely dependent on external orders—in this instance, God's commands—for your actions. In other words, when the Lord, through His word and Spirit, tells you to go here or there, you follow His leading. That is the whole plan; that is how God wants you to be.

> *"For as many as are led by the Spirit of God, they are the sons of God." (Romans 8:14)*

and the Psalmist affirms:

> *"Thy word is a lamp unto my feet and a light unto my path." (Psalm 119:105)*

The game plan is to do whatever God asks us to, and I pray God will get us all there in the name of Jesus Christ.

Let us not get it twisted; this has nothing to do with God tampering with your freewill. Instead, it is about understanding that subscribing to God's manual for your life guarantees the best results and performance in all you do. Nobody can ever lead or fix you better than your Maker. That is the point!

God's Zombie Blueprint works on the premise that:

## 1. JESUS KNOWS THE RIGHT STEP FOR YOU TO TAKE IN EVERY SITUATION

In **Psalms 23:1,** David wrote,

> *"The Lord is my shepherd, I shall not want."*

In the *New Century Version* (NCV), it reads:

> *"The Lord is my shepherd, I have everything I need."*

"I have everything I need"! Hallelujah! He takes care of your food and security requests; He takes care of all the decisions you need to make even as you take it to Him in prayer. It is as simple as that—a simple life! Just ask God about every step, and He makes your life easy.

You may be asking, "Who should I marry?" Well, did you not see what Adam did? When God created a wife for him by putting him into a deep sleep and brought forth Eve out of his ribs? The moment trouble came, and God asked him what had happened, Adam replied, "It is the wife you gave me!" So, you can ask God for anything, or He could give you something, but you should not go back to Him to say, "It is what you gave me that's causing me trouble!" Now, Adam's seed—that is, you and I—got out of trouble because God made a provision for our salvation by sending Jesus to come and die and make things right.

The point is God can get you out of any trouble whatsoever! Looking at Adam's story, he was in a bad jam, but he still got out of it because God made a way where there seemed to be none!

### 2. JESUS KNOWS WHAT YOU ARE GOING THROUGH

Apart from the fact that the Good Shepherd knows the terrain, the way, and the right step for you to take, He also knows precisely what you are going through every time. That is why His word says:

> "And it shall come to pass, that before they call, I will answer; and while they are yet speaking, I will hear." (**Isaiah 65:24**)

He knows! Even before you articulate your requests, God has an answer ready. Now, if He assures us that He will answer even before we call, why then do we still need to pray? Why are there delays in granting prayer requests? The truth is, He answers just as His word says. The problem is that we are often not *attentive* or sensitive enough to understand that He has responded. Talk about walking by the Spirit versus walking by sight! Thankfully, we will learn how to hear from God better as we proceed in this book (Chapter 8).

Believe me, if Jesus is the Shepherd that cares for you, and He is, and if you are truly following Him, then you can never go astray. When David wrote **Psalm 23** and proclaimed,

*When God is leading you, He provides for all your needs.*

*"The Lord is my shepherd,"*

he meant everything he was saying because he was a shepherd boy who took care of his father's sheep. David could empathize with what it takes to be a shepherd. That is why he wrote: "The Lord is my shepherd; I have everything I need…. Though I walk through the valley of the shadow of death, I will fear no evil, for thou art with me. Thy rod and thy staff, they comfort me."

In effect, David said to God, "I have confidence that you are powerful enough to keep the devil away. You are powerful enough to keep wolves away." That is why Scripture says,

> "He suffered no man to do them wrong. He reproved kings
> for their sake, saying touch not my anointed and do my
> prophet no harm." (**Psalm 105:14-15**)

God led Israel by putting His fear on all the nations around them, such that nobody could touch them. That is God for you. While He was guiding the Israelites, they never got into trouble because He suffered no man to do them wrong.

When God is leading you, He provides for all your needs. He is a great Shepherd, a Super One! He is the Good Shepherd. With Him, you can never miss your destination because he will sort everything out!

# Chapter 3

The Good Shepherd

# The Good Shepherd Cares for His Sheep

*Be not dismayed whate'er betide,*
*God will take care of you;*
*beneath his wings of love abide,*
*God will take care of you.*

*God will take care of you,*
*through every day, o'er all the way;*
*he will take care of you,*
*God will take care of you.*

*"God will take care of you" (1904)*

*by Civilla D. Martin, 1866-1948*

Y ou may want to ask, "Why does the Good Shepherd care for the sheep?" As human beings, sometimes, we want to understand 'the *why*', which is okay. So, let us take a closer look at **John 10:4-5.**

> *"And when he putteth forth his own sheep, he goeth before them, and the sheep follow him: for they know his voice. And a stranger will they not follow, but will flee from him: for they know not the voice of strangers."*

In this chapter, we shall address why the Good Shepherd cares for the sheep and how He cares for the sheep.

# WHY THE GOOD SHEPHERD CARES FOR THE SHEEP

Let us look at some reasons why the Good Shepherd cares for the sheep.

### 1. THE SHEEP ARE HIS

The Good Shepherd is not a hireling. He owns the sheep. So, the Lord cares because you belong to Him. In **John 10:12-13**, the scriptures state:

> *"But he that is an hireling, and not the shepherd, whose own the sheep are not, seeth the wolf coming, and leaveth the sheep, and fleeth: and the wolf catcheth them, and scattereth the sheep. ¹³The hireling fleeth, because he is an hireling, and careth not for the sheep."*

The hireling flees at the slightest sign of trouble, but not the shepherd. The Good Shepherd is committed to delivering the sheep from danger because the sheep belong to Him.

### 2. HE HAS INVESTED MUCH IN HIS FLOCK

God has invested so much in humankind. In **Psalm 8:4**, the Scripture says:

> *"What is man, that thou art mindful of him? and the son of*

*man, that thou visitest him?"*

**The Good Shepherd loves, and therefore, cares for His sheep.**

Here, the Psalmist imagines: 'How can You be so committed to man? What is he that You are mindful of him to the extent that You made him just a little lower than angels?'

In **Genesis 1:26**, the Bible tells us:

*"And God said, Let us make man in our image, after our likeness: and let them have dominion over the fish of the sea, and over the fowl of the air, and over the cattle, and over all the earth, and over every creeping thing that creepeth upon the earth."*

For every other thing created, God just spoke, 'Let there be this or that', and they came into being. But when it came to creating man, He did not follow the *'let there be'* pattern. God made us fearfully and wonderfully. God took His time to make you! He made you in the *likeness* of His *fullness*. That is why you are so valuable to God. He told Jeremiah:

*"Before I formed thee in the belly I knew thee; and before thou camest forth out of the womb I sanctified thee, and I ordained thee a prophet unto the nations. (**Jeremiah 1:5**)*

What God said to Jeremiah then, He is saying to you now! You are not just anybody; God has invested so much in you!

### 3. HE LOVES THE SHEEP

We all know the famous Scripture,

*"For God so loved the world… "(**John 3:16**)*

One thing stands out from that Scripture: if you love, then you must care.

Picture a scenario where a man tells his wife, "I love you". In the morning, she tells him that she has a headache, and he recommends she takes some pills and goes off to work. But when he returns home from work, he starts screaming, "Why is my food not served? You know I have to go to work for the family!" It is evident that he had forgotten that she had a headache! And what if it had gotten worse?

People who care do not act like that. That man's wife will consider the man's earlier profession of love to be false, and there is no way she will believe him any longer. If someone says that they love you, they must act in ways that prove they genuinely care because love shows genuine interest in someone else's affairs. Such is the love of God toward us! **Romans 8:35, 38-39** describes God's love as being so strong; we are inseparable from it.

One of the attributes of the Spirit of God is love. The Bible lists out the components of the fruit of the Spirit, starting with love:

> *"But the fruit of the Spirit is love, joy, peace, longsuffering, gentleness, goodness, meekness, temperance: against such there is no law." (**Galatians 5:22-23**).*

Of the nine characteristics of the fruit of the Spirit, the first and primary one is love, re-echoing the fact that God cares. He is not a man. Based on this truth, I do not doubt that Jesus cares!

# WHAT THE GOOD SHEPHERD DOES FOR THE SHEEP

Now, because the Good Shepherd cares, He does the following:

### 1. WHEN A SHEEP IS LOST, HE GOES AFTER THE SHEEP AND RE-STORES IT TO THE FOLD

God had a plan for humankind from the beginning before the devil came in and deceived man. In so doing, he sought to derail the divine masterplan. Ever since then, God has been working to get us, His sheep, back to the fold.

In the Prodigal Son's story, in **Luke 15:21-24**, the younger son had collected all his entitlements and had gone ahead to live wildly. But when he fell on hard times, he came to his senses and said to himself, "I will arise and go to my father." Once he got back home, there was so much excitement in the father that he threw a big party in celebration. There was rejoicing because the father cared. He had missed his son! Like the prodigal son, many people are living carelessly, and God is waiting. He is saying:

**The Good Shepherd**

*"Behold, I stand at the door* [the entrance of your heart],
*and knock: If any man hear my voice, and open the door,
I will come in to him, and will sup with him, and he with
me." (**Revelation 3:20**)*

God is waiting. He is in the business of restoring lives because He cares. I believe God is saying to you, "I am waiting for you!" He has invested too much in you, and He wants you to come back home.

In **John 8:1-11**, we read the story of a woman caught in adultery. Think about that; this was one of the lost sheep, caught in the very act of adultery. And according to the law of Moses, everybody was ready to stone her to death. But Jesus stooped down, and with His finger wrote on the ground, as though He heard them not. When they persisted, Jesus said,

*"He that is without sin among you, let him first cast a stone
at her." (**John 8:7**)*

One by one, all her accusers left, and the Bible relays what then transpired between the Lord and the woman:

*When Jesus had lifted up himself, and saw none but the
woman, he said unto her, Woman, where are those thine
accusers? hath no man condemned thee? She said, No man,
Lord. And Jesus said unto her, Neither do I condemn thee:
go, and sin no more. (**John 8:10-11**)*

Right there, He got another sheep back because He cares!

In another encounter, Jesus saw a man at the pool of Bethesda; for thirty-eight years, this man suffered from an incurable disease (**John 5:1-8**)! From the details of that encounter, we know that there was a great multitude of impotent folk who were blind, halt and withered, all waiting for the moving of the water. While I studied that portion of Scripture, the Lord opened my eyes to understand certain things about that man. First, he had the most significant problem of all the people who were there. You know why? He had been sick for a whooping thirty-eight years! Secondly, he was a sinner—he was *body sick* and *sin sick!* Then Jesus went to where he was and took his sickness away. And when Jesus saw him later, He said to him,

*Behold, thou art made whole: sin no more, lest a worse*

*thing come unto thee. (**John 5:14**)*

Why would Jesus take all that time to focus on that man? Because He cares!

Remember the woman of Samaria who encountered Jesus at the well? In **John 4:15-18**, we understand that she already had five husbands. And Jesus was talking to her! Imagine that in this day and time. Many would gossip, "We saw Pastor with that harlot. What was he saying to her?" But Jesus would go after every one to restore them to the fold because He cares. He is moved with compassion every time.

### 2. HE PROTECTS THE SHEEP FROM HARM

The Good Shepherd never gives up any sheep to wolves. **John 10** reveals this much. In **verses 12-13**, Jesus said:

> *"But he that is an hireling, and not the shepherd, whose own the sheep are not, seeth the wolf coming, and leaveth the sheep, and fleeth: and the wolf catcheth them, and scattereth the sheep. ¹³The hireling fleeth, because he is an hireling, and careth not for the sheep."*

Unlike the hireling, Jesus grants us protection. He says in **John 10:10**:

> *"The thief cometh not, but for to steal, and to kill, and to destroy: I am come that they might have life, and that they might have it more abundantly."*

In other words, He guarantees us protection. He led Israel from Egypt to the Promised Land. He took care of every one of them. In a strange terrain, He directed them. He put their fear on every nation around so that nobody could touch them. In **Exodus 23:20-23**, the LORD says:

> *"Behold, I send an Angel before thee, to keep thee in the way, and to bring thee into the place which I have prepared. ²¹Beware of him, and obey his voice, provoke him not; for he will not pardon your transgressions: for my name is in him. ²²But if thou shalt indeed obey his voice, and do all that I speak; then I will be an enemy unto thine enemies, and an adversary unto thine adversaries. ²³For mine Angel shall go before thee, and bring thee in unto the Amorites, and the*

*Hittites, and the Perizzites, and the Canaanites, the Hivites, and the Jebusites: and I will cut them off."*

He was in effect saying, if you will obey His voice and follow Him and do all that He commands and be a sheep, then He will be an enemy to your enemies and an adversary to your adversaries. That is why the Bible says,

*He suffered no man to do them wrong: yea, he reproved kings for their sakes; Saying, Touch not mine anointed, and do my prophets no harm. (**Psalms 105:14-15**)*

Because He cares, there is protection for you. In **Psalm 23:4**, the Bible says:

*"Yea, though I walk through the valley of the shadow of death, I will fear no evil: for thou art with me; thy rod and thy staff they comfort me."*

The Psalmist was not afraid because he had protection—divine protection!

*"I will lift up mine eyes unto the hills, from whence cometh my help. ²My help cometh from the Lord, which made heaven and earth. ³He will not suffer thy foot to be moved: he that keepeth thee will not slumber. ⁴Behold, he that keepeth Israel shall neither slumber nor sleep. ⁵The Lord is thy keeper: the Lord is thy shade upon thy right hand. ⁶The sun shall not smite thee by day, nor the moon by night. ⁷The Lord shall preserve thee from all evil: he shall preserve thy soul. ⁸The LORD shall preserve thy going out and thy coming in from this time forth, and even for evermore." (**Psalm 121:1-8**)*

All of that happens because the Lord is protecting you.

Let me share a true story that happened during the Second World War about a woman: Every night, jet fighters would drop bombs where she lived, shaking the homes there. So, she and everyone else in the neighbourhood fled from their homes to hide from the bombs. Her running to hide along with the neighbours continued until she read the Scripture where the Bible says,

*"He that keepeth Israel* [thee] *shall neither slumber nor sleep. ⁵The Lord is thy keeper." (Psalm 121:4-5a)*

When she saw it, she said to herself, if the One that keeps me neither slumbers nor sleep, why am I running away? From that day on, she never ran away from her home again!

Even though the fighter jets continued bombing the area, none of the blitzes came near her house! For three months, people thought she had died in the bombardment because she was not there whenever they ran to their usual shelter. One day she showed up, and they were all dazed. They asked to know of her whereabouts since she had not been sheltering with them, and she told them that, "He that keepeth me neither slumbers nor sleeps." Hallelujah!

Now, as a child of God today, if like that woman, He who keeps you does not slumber nor sleep, then why are you running? From what are you running? Have you not read in the Bible that,

*"He that dwelleth in the secret place of the most High shall abide under the shadow of the Almighty?" (Psalms 91:1)*

And in **Psalm 91:5-11,** the Psalmist states:

*"Thou shalt not be afraid for the terror by night; nor for the arrow that flieth by day; ⁶Nor for the pestilence that walketh in darkness; nor for the destruction that wasteth at noonday. ⁷A thousand shall fall at thy side, and ten thousand at thy right hand; but it shall not come nigh thee. ⁸Only with thine eyes shalt thou behold and see the reward of the wicked. ⁹Because thou hast made the Lord, which is my refuge, even the most High, thy habitation; ¹⁰There shall no evil befall thee, neither shall any plague come nigh thy dwelling. ¹¹For he shall give his angels charge over thee, to keep thee in all thy ways."*

This passage of Scripture means that stray arrows cannot locate you. Do you know what David said when Saul died? He asserted that Saul died as though God did not anoint him to be king. This kind of 'cheap' death shall not be your portion in Jesus' name, because the Bible says,

*"Touch not mine anointed. Do my prophet no harm."*

*(Psalm 105:15)*

The Bible records a conspiracy against the Israelites, where Balak sought to invoke a curse on them. The scriptures say that they called Balaam, a specialist in the area of cursing people, and said to him, "Curse this people, curse them!" And Balaam looked at Israel and tried in different places to curse them, all to no avail. Much to the dismay of Balak, instead of cursing them, Balaam began to proclaim thus:

> *"Surely there is no enchantment against Jacob, neither is there any divination against Israel: according to this time it shall be said of Jacob and of Israel, "What hath God wrought!"* (**Numbers 23:23**)

Did you see that? Balaam was opening his mouth to curse, but blessings were pouring out of his mouth instead! Believe me, whom God has blessed, no man can curse!

God declares with authority, *"Touch not mine anointed!"* because He cares, and that is why you are protected. The word of God says,

> *No weapon formed against thee shall prosper* (**Isaiah 54:17**).

### 3. HE PROVIDES FOR THE SHEEP

The Good Shepherd also goes by the name *Jehovah Jireh*—the Lord that provides. Do you know how He got this name? The Bible says that Abraham was to sacrifice his only son, Isaac, on the altar of obedience to God's command. And the boy asked, "Where is the animal we are going to kill for the sacrifice?" And Abraham responded to Isaac, saying, "The Lord will provide." After a 3-day journey on foot, Abraham finally got to the place for the sacrifice. By the time Abraham got to the appointed place, *Jehovah Jireh* had already provided a ram for the sacrifice (**Genesis 22:1**-14)!

This situation is like what many people face today, and they cry out, "Oh, I don't have a job." "I don't know where my next meal will come from!" Be aware that we are talking about Jehovah Jireh, the Creator of the whole earth. The silver and gold are His, and He cares for you!

We are talking about the God that fed six hundred thousand people, taking them through the wilderness. He fed them with manna, and when they asked for meat, He provided them with meat in excess. (**Exodus 16:1-18**).

Are you hungry and worried about your next meal? You need to hear what David had to say:

> *"I have been young, and now am old; yet have I not seen the righteous forsaken, nor his seed begging bread." (**Psalm 37:25**)*

I declare to you that an end has come to your begging for bread in the name of Jesus. You have entered your season of abundance!

In **Psalm 68:19**, the Bible says,

> *"Blessed be the Lord, who daily loadeth us with benefits, even the God of our salvation."*

He loads you daily with benefits because He cares. When one door closes, He opens another. When He opens a door, no man can shut it; and when He shuts a door, no man can open it! Part of the benefits of following God is that He has designed everything for your good.

> *All things are yours! (**1 Corinthians 3:21b**)*

In **Romans 8:28,** Scripture says:

> *"And we know that all things work together for good to them that love God, to them who are the called according to his purpose."*

The Good Shepherd will never leave you hungry. Never!

You need to get the right perspective about God. During a famine, He sent a raven to feed Elijah. There are different schools of thought about where the raven was getting the food; what matters is that God can use any means to execute His purpose. He can do it anyhow. He can even bring food directly from heaven, just so that He can feed His sheep.

I want you to live henceforth with the ever-abiding consciousness that God cares about you. Say to yourself as you go about your daily business: "Because God cares about me, I will not go hungry. He will take care of my family and me!"

Many people are worried sick thinking about tomorrow when God has already taken care of tomorrow. You are worried about too many things. But God said I should tell you through His word that every single hair on your head is accounted for.

Throughout the ages, humanity has always been consumed with thoughts of, "What will I eat?" "What will I wear?" "When will I do this or that," forgetting that God is the Provider, and He never fails.

Five thousand people were in a place, and Jesus said to Philip, "Get food so that we can feed these people." But there were only five loaves of bread and two small fishes, for five thousand people! You can imagine Philip telling Jesus that there was no market at that point where they could get enough food to feed that multitude. The Lord asked His disciples to tell the multitude to settle down; they did, were all fed, and even took up left-overs! (**John 6:5-13**; **Matthew 14:14-21**).

You will agree that settling down with just five loaves of bread and two small fishes requires some profound faith. There was nothing at all to see. It was evident that what was available could not feed all of them. But I implore you to act henceforth as that multitude of five thousand people because regardless of the 'reality', the Good Shepherd had said, "*Settle down!*" Like the 'reality' of that multitude then; today, the unemployment rate may be at an all-time high, but Jesus is telling you to "*Settle down!*" The economy might be going down, but Jesus is saying, "*Settle down!*" Just settle down and trust Him!

*If you must follow anyone, it must be the One who cared enough to die for you!*

If five thousand people could settle down for five loaves of bread and two small fishes, then your time has come. Your season of satisfaction has come in the name of Jesus. I declare to you that beginning from this moment, you are going to enjoy super-abundance. It is your season of unusual grace because God is your Provider, and He cares for you.

## 4. HE GAVE HIS LIFE FOR HIS SHEEP

Jesus gave His life for His sheep without being compelled. He gave it freely. He said:

> *"I lay down my life, that I might take it again. ¹⁸No man taketh it from me, but I lay it down of myself. I have power to lay it down, and I have power to take it again." (**John 10:17-18**)*

He says, "I gave up my life to purchase your own. I gave up my freedom so you can have yours. I gave up my wealth so that you can have yours." The life of a man is in the blood; hence, when Jesus died on the cross, He gave up everything—His blood, flesh; everything! He did all of that so that you can have it all.

> *"Surely he hath borne our griefs, and carried our sorrows: yet we did esteem him stricken, smitten of God, and afflicted. ⁵But he was wounded for our transgressions, he was bruised for our iniquities: the chastisement of our peace was upon him; and with his stripes we are healed." (**Isaiah 53:4-5**)*

To wound is to afflict; thus, they took His peace so that you can have yours. And He did it because He cares. He made all the provisions because He cares. Let me tell you; it cost Him everything!

Someone might be saying, "Oh, Jesus is not the first to be accused wrongly." Well, they may be right, but the difference with 'this Accused' is that He was willing to go and pay the price. When people are accused wrongly, the usual experience is that they would be crying and insisting that they did not commit the offence. But Christ willingly paid the price for the wrongful accusation. It was painful, but He was mindful of His calling as a Good Shepherd. It was so sad that the Bible recounts that when He got to the Garden of Gethsemane, He looked ahead to the cross and the pain and shame, and at that moment, He prayed aggressively asking,

> *Father, if thou be willing, remove this cup from me: nevertheless not my will, but thine, be done. (**Luke 22:42**)*

If God had removed the 'cup', you and I would be on our way to hell! Jesus prayed that prayer because He knew that the instant He took upon Himself the sins of humanity, the Father would turn His back on Him! It was that painful and costly! But because He cares, He surrendered, crying out, *"not my will, but thine, be done!"*

When Jesus hung on the cross, the filth of the sins of the world was upon Him. He was dying for the sins of adultery, fornication, lying, murder, malice, envy, bitterness, drunkenness, strife, seditions, and lasciviousness. Also, He was on the cross for the sins of idolatry, uncleanness, witchcraft, hatred, wrath, heresies, emulations, revelings, homosexuality, lesbianism, sorcery, greed, and stealing. Indeed, every known and unknown sin; every evil that men had ever done was upon Jesus on that cross! The Good Shepherd carried them all on our behalf! And because God, the Father, cannot behold iniquity, He could not look on Jesus on the cross with all that sin laid upon Him!

Christ suffered all of that so that the Father can help you and I. He cried on the cross,

> *"Eloi, Eloi, lama sabachthani?" which is being interpreted, My God, my God, why hast thou forsaken me?" (**Mark 15:34**)*

The sinless Lamb of God took upon Himself the sins of the whole world because He cares (**Mark 15:1-39**).

Therefore, if you must follow anyone, you had better follow the One who cared enough to lay down His life for you! If such a man says, *'follow me!'*, you had better follow Him because He will never lead you astray!

Concerning marriage, Scripture says,

> *"Wives, submit yourselves unto your own husbands, as unto the Lord." (**Ephesians 5:22**)*

and,

> *"Husbands, love your wives, even as Christ also loved the church, and gave himself for it" (**Ephesians 5:25**)*

Thus, the man should lead the wife, and the wife should follow!

Let me share a story with you to drive this home. I knew a woman who would not submit to her husband in any shape or form many years ago. She could not submit to his leadership because she was more affluent and earned more money than him. As a result of this, they often had fights. Then one day, they were travelling together from Lagos to Ibadan. On their way, armed robbers intercepted them, took all the woman's belongings, and decided that they would kill her. But the husband stepped forward, stood between the gun and his wife and told them: "You cannot kill my wife! If you must kill anybody, it has to be me first!" At that point, the robbers, stunned by the man's 'foolishness' mocked and called him, *a woman wrapper* which in local parlance means, "*a man who is being bossed around by his wife and would do anything to please her, even if it brought shame to him.*" The robbers then let them go, laughing at the man's 'folly'.

From that day on, the story of that couple changed. The wife realised that her husband—her head and leader—cared for her. He cared so much; he was willing to die for her!

Jesus was not just ready to die; He died for you and I. Therefore, if He tells you to *go left or go right*, you had better do so.

I challenge you to become God's *'zombie'*—become God-controlled—from this day forward, and you can rest assured that you cannot go wrong in life. That is why David said,

> "*The Lord is my Shepherd, I have everything I need.*"
> (**Psalm 23:1, NCV**)

May you come to that level of understanding, in Jesus name.

# Chapter 4

The Good Shepherd

# The Good Shepherd Knows His Sheep

*I have a Maker*

*He formed my heart*

*Before even time began*

*My life was in His Hands*

*He knows my name*

*He knows my every thought*

*He sees each tear that falls*

*And He hears me when I call*

*"He Knows My Name" (2000)*

*by Tommy Walker*

*"I am the good shepherd, and know my sheep, and am known of mine" (**John 10:14**)*

In the text above, Jesus introduces us to a vital aspect of His nature as the Good Shepherd; the fact that *He is Omniscient*—that is, He is infinite in knowledge. He has complete knowledge and awareness of everything! He knows all things! **Daniel 2:20-22** gives us some insight:

*"Daniel answered and said, Blessed be the name of God for ever and ever: for wisdom and might are his: [21]And he changeth the times and the seasons: he removeth kings, and setteth up kings: he giveth wisdom unto the wise, and knowledge to them that know understanding: [22]He revealeth the deep and secret things: he knoweth what is in the darkness, and the light dwelleth with him."*

## THE ALL-KNOWING SHEPHERD

The outward appearance of an individual can deceive human beings but not God! In **1 Samuel 16:6-7**, when Samuel was sent to Jesse's house to anoint a king, he saw Eliab, the firstborn and was moved to think that Eliab was the chosen one. Samuel assumed that Eliab was the person God had chosen because of his countenance—height and physique. However, God told Samuel clearly that He had rejected Eliab. The Good Shepherd knows His sheep! Choosing David was never about human parameters; it came from a place of divine knowledge.

The thing about God as the Good Shepherd, and you as His sheep, is that *He knows* your totality. *Jesus knows* the sheep; therefore, He cannot be deceived! As humans or as leaders, we can lead people for many years and still not know them. But *the Good Shepherd* is different—*He is Omniscient*—He knows what you are doing at all times.

We shall discuss the omniscience dimension of the Good Shepherd's attributes under four headings:

1. He knows your name
2. He knows your thoughts

3. He knows your personality
4. He knows what you are going through

So, let's look at each of these parts now.

### 1. THE GOOD SHEPHERD KNOWS YOUR NAME

Scripture is replete with instances of the demonstration of God's all-knowing power. In **John 1:47-48**, the Bible tells us of how Nathanael became Jesus' disciple:

> *Jesus saw Nathanael coming to him, and saith of him, "Behold an Israelite indeed, in whom is no guile!" [48]Nathanael saith unto him, Whence knowest thou me? Jesus answered and said unto him," Before that Philip called thee, when thou wast under the fig tree, I saw thee."*

Nathanael needed no further convincing after he had encountered Someone who knew him even before meeting him one-on-one.

Similarly, in **Exodus 3:4,** Scripture reveals how God called Moses out of the burning bush by name. In **1 Samuel 3:4**, He called Samuel by name. In **Luke 19:5**, He called Zacchaeus by name. The list goes on and on. The point is, God knows each person's name as distinct from another, implying that if ten people bear the same name, God knows each one of them distinctly from the others. He will not mistake one for the other.

*The Good Shepherd knows everything about everyone and everything else!*

Of course, the case will be quite different in the secular where the leader will certainly have a hard time differentiating one individual from another. But not so with God! Regardless of how far science has gone, man is extremely limited in knowledge, but God is unlimited. God knows everyone distinctly and cannot mistake one person for the other even when they bear the same name.

There are certain spiritual privileges you enjoy as a Christian because God knows your name:

- No charmer can use your name for charms.
- No enchanter can put a spell on you.
- No adversary can raise an altar of affliction against you.

Also, because you are God's sheep, you are not permitted to bear a name that does not glorify Him. For example, you cannot have a name that starts with "*Esu*" (meaning devil in the Yoruba language). How can God call you by such a name? Hence, once you are born again, you are expected to drop any name that glorifies Satan! We live in a world where people erroneously believe that individual gifts and fortunes come from specific deities, so parents name their children based on this belief. On the contrary, your identity as a child of God must resonate with His purpose for your life.

## 2. THE GOOD SHEPHERD KNOWS YOUR THOUGHTS

Let us take a look at what Scripture says in **Psalm 139:1-13**:

> *"LORD, thou hast searched me, and known me. ²Thou knowest my downsitting and mine uprising, thou understandest my thought afar off. ³Thou compassest my path and my lying down, and art acquainted with all my ways. ⁴For there is not a word in my tongue, but, lo, O Lord, thou knowest it altogether. ⁵Thou hast beset me behind and before, and laid thine hand upon me. ⁶Such knowledge is too wonderful for me; it is high, I cannot attain unto it. ⁷Whither shall I go from thy spirit? Or whither shall I flee from thy presence? ⁸If I ascend up into heaven, thou art there: if I make my bed in hell, behold, thou art there. ⁹If I take the wings of the morning, and dwell in the uttermost parts of the sea; ¹⁰Even there shall thy hand lead me, and thy right hand shall hold me. ¹¹If I say, Surely the darkness shall cover me; even the night shall be light about me. ¹²Yea, the darkness hideth not from thee; but the night shineth as the day: the darkness and the light are both alike to thee. ¹³For thou hast possessed my reins: thou hast covered me in my mother's womb."*

The Psalmist could not help but exclaim, "*Such knowledge is too wonderful for me!*" That is precisely what happens when you grasp the 'all-knowing' aspect of the Good Shepherd's character.

He is the God who knows everything about everyone and everything else! In the story of Jonah and his assignment at Nineveh, the Bible makes us understand that when Jonah repented in the belly of the fish and the Lord saw his heart, that God instructed the fish to vomit him on dry ground (**Jonah 2:1-10**)!

Because God sees all men's hearts, He was able to see Jonah's heart that he was genuinely repentant.

We see another example in **Genesis 6:5**, where Scripture says:

> *"And GOD saw that the wickedness of man was great in the earth, and that every imagination of the thoughts of his heart was only evil continually."*

God knows every imagination of your heart—every single one of them!

Get this: no man or court could have been able to prosecute David for his actions against Uriah except God, who sees the heart. When David plotted and executed his evil plan, he thought he would go scot-free because, in his mind, no one knew about it. How wrong he was! God sent His servant, Nathan, and gave David a grim picture of his offence. In his ignorance, David sought to punish the character in Nathan's illustration but ended up passing judgment on himself. That is what happens when a man tries to play smart with the *All-knowing God*. Nothing can be concealed from God.

> *"And the Lord sent Nathan unto David. And he came unto him, and said unto him, There were two men in one city; the one rich, and the other poor. ²The rich man had exceeding many flocks and herds: ³But the poor man had nothing, save one little ewe lamb, which he had bought and nourished up: and it grew up together with him, and with his children; it did eat of his own meat, and drank of his own cup, and lay in his bosom, and was unto him as a daughter. ⁴And there came a traveler unto the rich man, and he spared to take of his own flock and of his own herd, to dress for the wayfaring man that was come unto him; but took the poor man's lamb, and dressed it for the+ man that was come to him. ⁵And David's anger was greatly kindled against the man; and he said to Nathan, As the Lord liveth, the man that hath done this thing shall surely die: ⁶And he shall restore the lamb fourfold, because he did this thing, and because he had no pity. ⁷And Nathan said to David, Thou art the man. Thus saith the Lord God of Israel, I anointed thee king over Israel, and I delivered thee out of the hand of*

*Saul; ⁸And I gave thee thy master's house, and thy master's wives into thy bosom, and gave thee the house of Israel and of Judah; and if that had been too little, I would moreover have given unto thee such and such things. ⁹Wherefore hast thou despised the commandment of the Lord, to do evil in his sight? thou hast killed Uriah the Hittite with the sword, and hast taken his wife to be thy wife, and hast slain him with the sword of the children of Ammon. ¹⁰Now therefore the sword shall never depart from thine house; because thou hast despised me, and hast taken the wife of Uriah the Hittite to be thy wife. ¹¹Thus saith the Lord, Behold, I will raise up evil against thee out of thine own house, and I will take thy wives before thine eyes, and give them unto thy neighbour, and he shall lie with thy wives in the sight of this sun. ¹²For thou didst it secretly: but I will do this thing before all Israel, and before the sun. ¹³And David said unto Nathan, I have sinned against the Lord. And Nathan said unto David, The Lord also hath put away thy sin; thou shalt not die. ¹⁴Howbeit, because by this deed thou hast given great occasion to the enemies of the Lord to blaspheme, the child also that is born unto thee shall surely die."* (**2 Samuel 12:1-14**)

As a child of God, you must understand that He knows your thoughts, which means that you cannot afford to harbour sin in your heart when you pray. **Psalms 66:18** says:

> *"If I regard iniquity in my heart, the Lord will not hear me."*

When you look at a woman lustfully, for instance, the Lord sees your heart (**Matthew 5:28**). He answers the *"effectual fervent prayer"* (**James 5:16**) because it is a prayer from the heart. He sees and knows the thoughts and imaginations of our hearts (**Psalm 37:4**)!

### 3. THE GOOD SHEPHERD KNOWS YOUR PERSONALITY

Your personality is the totality of your physical, mental, emotional, and social attributes. The Psalmist says,

> *"I will praise thee; for I am fearfully and wonderfully made: marvelous are thy works; and that my soul knoweth right well."*(**Psalm 139:14**)

God made us, and He knows everything about our being. For example, He knew Job's personality, so He boasted about Job to the devil (**Job 1:8-11**). He could not say the same for many of the children of Israel. Moses, their leader, had hardly gone up the mountain to meet God when they had moved on to worship the gold calf! They could not tarry for Moses' return. They turned their back on God and switched to worshipping idols in under forty days!

God trusted that Abraham would teach his children the way of the Lord (**Genesis 18:19**), but He could not say the same for Eli, who did not bring up his children to fear the Lord (**1 Samuel 2:12-17, 22-36**).

God sent His prophet to the widow of Zarephath because He trusted her (**1 Kings 17:9**). He looked many miles away from Cherith, even when there were widows in Israel, yet God did not trust them to deliver on the assignment regarding His servant, Elijah.

God trusted Joshua and Caleb to give a good report concerning the Promise Land. Twelve men searched out the land, but God already knew that only these two men would deliver good news. It did not matter what the others said.

From Scripture's authority, we can see that the Good Shepherd knows every one of His sheep—both the saved and lost sheep! He knows your name, your thoughts, and your personality—He knows everything about you!

### 4. THE GOOD SHEPHERD KNOWS WHAT YOU ARE GOING THROUGH

The Good Shepherd also knows what you are going through. In **Isaiah 65:24**, God says:

> *"And it shall come to pass, that before they call, I will answer; and while they are yet speaking, I will hear."*

God will answer even before you ask because He knows what you will ask! In **John 11:11**, Lazarus was dead, and Jesus knew that. In **John 11:14**, Jesus confirmed to His disciples that he already knew about Lazarus' death. In **Luke 13:15-16**, we read the story about a woman bound for eighteen years. Without anybody telling Him, Jesus knew aforehand that she had been in that condition for those number of years! Indeed,

---

God knows what you are going through.

In **Exodus 3:7-11**, God spoke to Moses, telling him that He knew about the affliction the children of Israel had been suffering in Egypt for several years:

> *"And the LORD said, 'I have surely seen the affliction of my people which are in Egypt, and have heard their cry by reason of their taskmasters; for I know their sorrows; ⁸And I am come down to deliver them out of the hand of the Egyptians, and to bring them up out of that land unto a good land and a large, unto a land flowing with milk and honey; unto the place of the Canaanites, and the Hittites, and the Amorites, and the Perizzites, and the Hivites, and the Jebusites. ⁹Now therefore, behold, the cry of the children of Israel is come unto me: and I have also seen the oppression wherewith the Egyptians oppress them. ¹⁰Come now therefore, and I will send thee unto Pharaoh, that thou mayest bring forth my people the children of Israel out of Egypt.' ¹¹And Moses said unto God, 'Who am I, that I should go unto Pharaoh, and that I should bring forth the children of Israel out of Egypt?"*

God said, *"I have also seen…"*; in other words, he knew much more than the outcry of His people from their burdens. He was very much aware of the whole situation.

*There is an exciting touch to the all-knowing dimension of the Good Shepherd; He does not remember your "repented sin!"*

Similarly, in **1 Kings 19:4-8**, He intercepted Elijah on his way and told him to rise and eat because the journey ahead was very demanding. He knew just what Elijah was going through—the prophet was highly discouraged, and God showed up to encourage him!

The Good Shepherd had to pass through Samaria because of the woman He needed to meet by the well. He knew her story and the life she was living. He also knew how His encounter with her would radically transform her life, and turn her into a vessel of honour, as she began to spread the glad tidings about the Messiah—a Man Who knew all she ever did (**John 4:28-29**)!

In **John 5:5-8**, Jesus knew that the man at the pool called Bethesda had been sick for thirty-eight years. That is why He walked straight to him and restored him.

In all, the Good Shepherd's all-knowing attribute should inspire you to have implicit trust in His ability to lead, protect and provide for you! He knows everything about you—the things you are going through, your challenges, fears, and heart's desires. He also knows your short-comings; when you are telling a lie and when you are planning evil. He knows when you are living a hypocritical life and when you are playing church. *He knows them all!*

Little wonder the Bible says that it is a fearful thing to fall into the hands of the living God (**Hebrews 11:31**). It is frightening for your enemies because they cannot touch you. It is terrifying for you because you cannot hide anything from Him. Imagine someone calling you and saying that he knows all your details and plans—your bank details, vital documents, secrets, your next move, everything! Would you not be afraid of such a person? Of course, you would! You would not dare annoy or disobey that person. You would do whatever it takes to be in their good books. And if you wanted to go after that individual, to eliminate the threat they pose, you would immediately fall in line when something drastic happens to your details because the individual was aware aforehand of your move!

Fortunately for you and I, that Person who has all your 'info' at His fingertips is the loving God about whom we have been speaking! While He will not hold you to ransom as a man would, given all that power over you, Scripture still warns us that it is a fearful thing to fall into His hands because He holds the key to your life! Rather than play games with God, it is in your best interest to stand in awe of Him!

# THE ONE THING GOD DOES NOT REMEMBER

Is there something that can escape the "all-knowing" God's memory? Well, none literally. But there is an exciting touch to the all-knowing dimension of the Good Shepherd; He does not remember your "repented sin!"

That is right! When you repent of any sin, God forgets all about it completely!

> *"I, even I, am he that blotteth out thy transgressions for mine own sake, and will not remember thy sins."( Isaiah 43:25-26)*

**Hebrews 10:17** also affirms this:

> *"And their sins and iniquities will I remember no more"*

These scripture passages imply that if you were to see God today and ask Him what the last sin you confessed was, He would not remember. That is why He says, I forgive you, and I remember your sins no more. What a God!

Imagine if God were to remember all our sins; no man would stand a chance in His court of judgment, for the Bible says that the heart of man always purposes to do evil continually. But because He is a merciful God, He chooses to be *'all-unknowing'* in recalling repented sins, though He is the all-knowing God. God deserves nothing less than our obedience and gratitude. He pays attention to what is virtuous and better about us. Little wonder the Psalmist says,

> *"If thou, LORD, shouldest mark iniquities, O Lord, who shall stand?" (Psalm 130:3)*

No one can stand because His word tells us that our righteousness or morality are like filthy rags before Him (**Isaiah 64:6**).

Praise be to God, Who knows everything about us. He leads, protects, and provides for us (His sheep) while choosing to forgive and forget our past transgressions, which we have confessed and forsaken. Hallelujah!

# PART TWO

## *Characteristics of The Sheep:*

*Relationship Dimensions with The Good Shepherd*

# TABLE OF CONTENTS FOR PART TWO

# Chapter 5

**The Good Shepherd**

# The Following Dimension

*"Take up thy cross and follow Me,"*
*I heard my Master say;*
*"I gave My life to ransom thee,*
*Surrender your all today."*

*Wherever He leads I'll go.*

*Wherever He leads I'll go.*

*I'll follow my Christ who loves me so,*

*Wherever He leads I'll go*


*"Wherever He leads I'll go" (1936)*

*by B.B. McKinney, 1886-1952*

B y the allegory in **John 10**, we see the following characteristics in the sheep:

1. They *follow* the Good Shepherd
2. They *trust* the Good Shepherd
3. They *know* the Good Shepherd
4. They *know the voice* of the Good Shepherd

In this chapter, we shall focus on the characteristic of the sheep following the Good Shepherd. Before we delve into that, though, let me point out the relational aspects of the sheep and the Good Shepherd.

# THE SHEEP AND THE GOOD SHEPHERD

### THE GOOD SHEPHERD

The Good Shepherd is not a man, which is a very weighty remark deserving of our attention. The Bible says of God not being a man thus:

> *God is not a man, that he should lie; neither the son of man, that he should repent: hath he said, and shall he not do it? or hath he spoken, and shall he not make it good? (Num-bers 23:19)*

Because the Good Shepherd is not a man, He cannot lie, neither is He inconsistent. He is unchanging and, therefore, consistent. The following qualities are proof of the Good Shepherd's consistency:

- He has Integrity: He does not waiver.

> *Every good gift and every perfect gift is from above, and cometh down from the Father of lights, with whom is no variableness, neither shadow of turning. (James 1:17)*

> *Jesus Christ the same yesterday, and to day, and for ever. (Hebrews 13:8)*

- He is Reliable: Anything God says that will He do. If God knew yesterday, He still knows today. Nothing changes about Him.

*... hath he [God] said, and shall he not do it? or hath he spoken, and shall he not make it good? (**Numbers 23:19**)*

*... the Strength of Israel will not lie nor repent: for he is not a man, that he should repent. (**1 Samuel 15:29**)*

- He is the Unchangeable Changer: He can change everything, but nothing can change Him!

*For I am the LORD, I change not; therefore ye sons of Jacob are not consumed. (**Malachi 3:6**)*

- He is Consistent: He will never fail or disappoint you. The word 'faithful' can only truly be used in the context of God because men are not faithful.

*God is faithful, by whom ye were called unto the fellowship of his Son Jesus Christ our Lord. (**1 Corinthians 1:9**)*

*If we believe not, yet he abideth faithful: he cannot deny himself. (**2 Timothy 2:13**)*

- He is Holy: That is His nature.

*Speak unto all the congregation of the children of Israel, and say unto them, Ye shall be holy: for I the LORD your God am holy. (**Leviticus 19:2**)*

*But as he which hath called you is holy, so be ye holy in all manner of conversation; ¹⁶Because it is written, Be ye holy; for I am holy. (**1 Peter 1:15-16**)*

- He is Capable: Nothing is too complicated that He cannot resolve! He can do whatever is impossible with men! There is no burden or situation that He cannot handle.

*Is any thing too hard for the LORD? At the time appointed I will return unto thee, according to the time of life, and Sarah shall have a son. (**Genesis 18:14**)*

*For with God nothing shall be impossible. (**Luke 1:37**)*

Everything we have mentioned about the Good Shepherd in Part One of this book cannot change because they are fixed. In mathematical terms, we can conclude that: the characteristics of the Good Shepherd are a constant! You can call Him the Constant One!

Now, let us talk about sheep.

## THE SHEEP

The sheep are human beings who are born again and sanctified by the Spirit of God and can thus follow the Good Shepherd obediently. Besides sheep, other human beings there are, with the tendency to manifest one characteristic now, only to switch to a directly contrary nature in the twinkling of an eye! These other human beings are thus incapable of following the Good Shepherd.

To grasp what led David, as sheep, to repose such confidence in the Good Shepherd as evident in **Psalm 23,** we need to understand the difference between the sheep described by Jesus in **John 10** and other human beings.

# FOLLOWING THE GOOD SHEPHERD

The sheep described by Jesus in **John 10** are sheep that *"follow"* the Shepherd. You must understand this aspect of the sheep *following* the Shepherd so that your benefit in following the Good Shepherd can be guaranteed. Hence, we ought to pay particular attention to what it takes to follow the Good Shepherd.

## WHAT DOES IT MEAN TO FOLLOW THE GOOD SHEPHERD?

To follow means to be utterly dependent on the one you are following. Concerning the Good Shepherd, it means to be utterly dependent on Him for your life, including your provision, protection, and preservation. In **John 15:5b,** Jesus Christ, the Good Shepherd, said:

*"Without me ye can do nothing!"*

Since sheep cannot do anything without their shepherd, they are dependent on him. Without a shepherd, the sheep will die! The sheep understand that without the shepherd, they are lost!

You need to understand that you cannot take any step without that person leading you. In other words, you cannot make decisions without the one that is leading—you have to depend on them.

The most sophisticated way of making decisions from a technical standpoint is vastly available in the secular world. One decision-making approach weighs the options open to you against the attendant results or benefits accruing from each of those options. The more accrued benefits, the better the choice. Another decision-making approach is that of probability. Here, you base your decision by looking at two different options, and then you weigh it by the likelihood of it occurring. It entails that you ask: "What is the probability that this or that would happen?" before finally deciding on which way to go. However, you will not survive this life using these techniques. If the world's sophisticated decision-making models were failsafe, then the great economies of the world that have collapsed would not have!

*You can call the Good Shepherd The Constant One because His attributes are unchanging!*

There have been times when countries like the United States of America have posted a meagre annual GDP (Gross Domestic Product) growth of just one per cent. The United Kingdom had published less than one per cent—and these with all that massive technology at their disposal! It is thus clear that we need more than technology to succeed. You cannot base your decisions on economic theories because there are unknown factors to man and beyond human control. That is why it is critical to follow the Good Shepherd!

Many people in the world today are suffering because they are following shepherds other than the Good Shepherd. And I am not just talking about secular people. Many follow God up to a point, even in the Church, and then switch to follow another shepherd.

I will give you an example of what I'm trying to say. Once, Jesus asked His disciples,

> *Whom do men say that I the Son of man am? ... whom say ye that I am? (**Matthew 16:13, 15**)*

Peter responded thus:

> *Thou art the Christ, the Son of the living God. (**Matthew 16:16**)*

Jesus looked at him and said,

> *Blessed art thou, Simon Barjona: for flesh and blood hath not revealed it unto thee, but my Father which is in heaven. (**Matthew 16:17**)*

In other words, He said that Peter was following the Spirit of God, for what he said could only have been revealed to him by the Spirit of God!

Based on Peter's response, Jesus then decided to give them more information about His mission on Earth. He reasoned that if the Holy Spirit had already revealed to Peter that He was the Son of God, then, He could go ahead and give them more details. He then went on and told them that He was going to die and will rise again. But Peter could not absorb that information. "No! You will not die!" he scolded Jesus. At this, Jesus rebuked Him saying,

> *Get thee behind me, Satan (**Matthew 16:23**)*

Did you see that? The same individual, who received an accolade just before then, was being rebuked sharply for speaking against the will of God. One minute, Peter was inspired by the Holy Spirit and the very next moment, Satan was influencing him!

Right there, we can see how easily one could be 'led' (influenced) by two different personalities—one good and one evil—within minutes!

### THE KEY TO EFFECTIVE FOLLOWERSHIP

From Jesus' response to Peter in **Matthew 16:23**, it is clear that some factors are involved when you are following someone.

1. To follow the Good Shepherd effectively, you need to be spiritual and sensitive to the Holy Spirit. Otherwise, you will go astray without even knowing it because numerous voices abound in the spirit realm. The same man who confessed Jesus to be the Son of God by the Holy Spirit turns around to oppose the crucial part of His mission on earth—which was to die and rise again on the third day—because he listened to another voice—the voice of the devil! The devil craftily blind-

ed Peter from the fact that Jesus was to rise again on the third day! Instead, Peter's heart straightaway rejected the idea of Jesus dying but did not consider that He would rise again on the third day!

The dying part did not appeal to Peter. He probably was thinking, "Come on, Jesus, how can you die?" Peter must have concluded that the dying part came from the pit of hell and immediately interrupted Him, "Jesus, you cannot die!" But Jesus sharply rebuked Peter for speaking words inspired by Satan. Those who seek to stop the work of God have opened themselves to Satan's influence!

2.   To follow the Good Shepherd, you cannot rationalize things as natural men do! Some people tend to think in a cause-and-effect manner; that is, "If I do something that seems to work, it is because I did something right." But that may not be the case—it is not about what you do; it is about following the Good Shepherd! We all always tend to miss this point. Like Peter, we tend to think that "If it is good, it is God; if it is not good, it is not God!"

That is not how to follow the Good Shepherd. When things seem to be working our way, we tend to think, "I must have done something right", but the truth is, nobody sent them to do those things. The scriptures make this so clear when Jesus told His disciples that at the time of judgment, many would say,

> Lord, Lord, have we not prophesied in thy name? and in thy name have cast out devils? and in thy name done many wonderful works? (**Matthew 7:22**)

But Jesus said that He would say to them.

> I never knew you: depart from me, ye that work iniquity. (**Matthew 7:23**)

Think about it. Why would Jesus tell them that? The truth is, many a times, people do things that God did not send them to do. At such times, we must ask ourselves, "Who am I following?"

## ESTABLISHING THE SHEEP-SHEPHERD CONNECTION

God created human beings to follow Him, but when Adam and Eve disobeyed Him by listening to Satan, Satan became their new shepherd. There is a God-void in humanity that cannot be satisfied by following anyone else. Following is a default programme ingrained in man. It is just so sad that many would follow anything but the One Who matters.

The farther they drift from Him, the greater their need of Him. What then does it take to establish the sheep-shepherd connection? First, you must have a spiritual relationship with the Good Shepherd—to follow means that you have to be born again.

> *Jesus answered and said unto him, Verily, verily, I say unto thee, Except a man be born again, he cannot see the king-dom of God … Except a man be born of water and of the Spirit, he cannot enter into the kingdom of God. That which is born of the flesh is flesh; and that which is born of the Spirit is spirit. (**John 3:3-6**)*

If a human being wants to follow God, Who is a Spirit, that individual must have a spiritual connection to Him, and this is where being born again comes into play. When we get to discussing *knowing His voice* in a subsequent chapter, it will open your insight into how to recognize the voice of God and understand how to follow Him.

In the light of our discussion, let me throw some light on **Romans 10:17.**

> *So then faith cometh by hearing, and hearing by the word of God.*

Faith comes by hearing—hearing God's word—yet many of God's peo-ple who frequently listen to His word still do not have faith. Why does that happen? It happens because they do not recognize the voice of God while listening to a message in a fellowship or when reading the Bible by themselves! For instance, if God were to say to you, "Go jump off a bridge", you would do it if you knew that it was God speaking. But if you have never heard from God, nor are intimate with His character, then you will not know if He is the One leading you! I assure you that if you truly *hear* from God, you will gladly do what He says. And the good news is that it is possible to hear from God directly while listening to a message in a church meeting or reading the Bible all by yourself.

Scripture records how Joshua had always *followed* Moses as a leader but had never heard directly from God on his own before. All Joshua knew was that Moses went up the mountain to speak with God and returned with a message from God. And then Moses dies! At that point, the importance of hearing from God personally hit home. I can imagine Joshua sitting down, sad and crying because he did not know what to do. Suddenly, God said: "*Arise!*" If you ever wondered how a servant would wake up one day and suddenly lead Israel, I will tell you how: Joshua heard from God!

When you start hearing from God, your faith will arise; your life will change, and you will never query what He tells you again! If God says that something is going to happen, it will happen!

I recall an incident that occurred one time in one of the organizations I worked for: precisely on July 31 of that year. By August of the same year, I heard from God! He told me that I was not going down as a result of that problem. But a month later, someone came and told me they had sacked me, that he was aware that the company had written my sack letter.

"You mean me?" I asked him. Within me, I said, "I don't think this one knows who he is talking about." I had confidence that his report was false because I had heard from God on the matter. I could not have heard from God and then believe a man! The rumour had it that they tore the sack letter twice! "Why?" you may wonder. It is because God had spoken on the matter, and He had assured me that there was nothing to fear.

You must understand that to *follow* the Good Shepherd is at a *spiritual level*. Therefore, the sheep must follow, trust, and know Him. They must also know His voice to have confidence that when He speaks, it is done. They would not have to wait to see things happen before believing that it is done. They would believe that since God has spoken, it is done!

Many years ago, my son was sick with pneumonia. He was about four months old at the time. So, we went to the hospital. We kept asking ourselves, "What is this?" My wife was on admission with him in the hospital; meanwhile, I asked God what He would have me do? Then, I left the hospital and went home.

When I got home, I got down on the floor in my room, and I immersed myself in reading the Bible. Then, I heard God say, *"Go thy way, thy son liveth!"* Instantly, I got up and was screaming with joy. Anyone who heard would think I had gone mad. Then I went to the hospital and told my wife that there was no problem anymore. The reality was that our son's condition had not changed, but I assured her that God had taken care of things. Three days later, the hospital discharged them! Believe me, once you hear from God, the problem is over!

I pray that you will get to know *how to hear from God* so that you can move to the next level of intimacy with Him.

*The sheep must know the Good Shepherd's voice to be confident that when He speaks, it is done.*

The critical thing to understand is that to follow the Shepherd, you first must be born again. When you are born again and sanctified, you become His sheep, and your spirit comes alive to God, thus making you willing to do His will wholeheartedly.

Scripture makes us understand that it is a tragedy when a man stops following God. The moment you are not doing God's will wholeheartedly, it means that you have stopped following Him. It is like when God asked King Saul to wipe out the whole of Amalek, but Saul chose to spare some of them. It was clearly against God's instruction, and God's verdict was not pleasant for king Saul.

> *"Then came the word of the LORD unto Samuel, saying,*
> [11]*"It repenteth me that I have set up Saul to be king: for he is turned back from following me, and hath not performed my commandments." And it grieved Samuel; and he cried unto the LORD all night." (**1 Samuel 15:10-11**)*

As His sheep, therefore, following God—the Good Shepherd means:

### DOING HIS WILL, ONE HUNDRED PER CENT—WHOLEHEARTEDLY!

> *Amaziah was twenty-five years old when he became king and reigned twenty-nine years in Jerusalem. His mother was Jehoaddin from Jerusalem. ²He lived well before GOD, doing the right thing for the most part. But he wasn't wholeheartedly devoted to God ... ¹⁴On his return from the destruction of the Edomites, Amaziah brought back the gods*

*of the men of Seir and installed them as his own gods, wor-*
*shiping them and burning incense to them. ¹⁵That ignited*
*GOD's anger; a fiery blast of GOD's wrath put into words*
*by a God-sent prophet: "What is this? Why on earth would*
*you pray to inferior gods who couldn't so much as help*
*their own people from you—gods weaker than Amaziah?"*
*(2 Chronicles 25: 1-2, 14-15, MSG)*

How could a man claiming to be following God turn around to worship and pay obeisance to the idols that could not save the nation that
worshipped it? The kingdom that he conquered with the help of God?
When we do not serve God wholeheartedly, we only follow Him when
we are in trouble; but when things are fine, we follow another.

### PLEASING HIM

*Can two walk together, except they be agreed? (Amos 3:3)*

You must fall in line with God because He is Constant. As men, the responsibility is on us to change to become like Him. It is a prerequisite for
the *sheep-shepherd connection.*

### BEING LED BY HIM

*"For as many as are led by the Spirit of God, they are the*
*sons of God." (Romans 8:14)*

### YOU HAVE TO BE HOLY

*But as he which hath called you is holy, so be ye holy in all*
*manner of conversation; ¹⁶Because it is written, Be ye holy;*
*for I am holy. (1 Peter 1:15-16)*

Holiness and total obedience are required if you must follow God.

When you follow the Good Shepherd wholeheartedly by pleasing Him,
being led by the Holy Spirit, and living a holy life, you will undoubtedly
see God!

*"Follow peace with all men, and holiness, without which no*
*man shall see the Lord."( Hebrews 12:14)*

---

And this is what guarantees eternal life!

# THE BENEFITS OF FOLLOWING THE GOOD SHEPHERD

*"My sheep hear my voice, and I know them, and they follow me: [28]And I give unto them eternal life; and they shall never perish, neither shall any man pluck them out of my hand. [29]My Father, which gave them me, is greater than all; and no man is able to pluck them out of my Father's hand."(-* **John 10:27-29)**

From the above scripture passage, we see the assurance that Jesus gives to those who follow Him. These assurances or guarantees are:

## 1. ETERNAL LIFE

When you follow the Good Shepherd, you are guaranteed eternal life. Do you remember one of the thieves who was crucified along with Jesus at Calvary? The one who said,

> *Lord, remember me when thou comest into thy kingdom.* **(Luke 23:42)**

Jesus guaranteed him eternal life:

> *Verily I say unto thee, To day shalt thou be with me in paradise.* **(Luke 23:43)**

What an assurance! What a great escape for that thief! How much more if you decide to follow Him from now on!

What a fortunate 'thief'! What a rare opportunity to repent at a dying moment! He grabbed eternal salvation just like that because he decided *to follow* Christ at the last minute! And Jesus said unto him,

> *"Verily I say unto thee, Today shalt thou be with me in paradise."* **(Luke 23: 43)**.

Wow, what an assurance! The lesson here is that faith in Jesus guarantees eternal life!

Jesus' message while on earth was about salvation based on faith in Him and nothing else. The thief on the cross demonstrated faith in Jesus. Even though Jesus was then being subjected to a shameful death on the cross with common thieves like him, he still believed in Jesus as the Saviour and asked to be with Him in His glory. He had faith in Jesus enough to follow Him even after Jesus had been beaten, battered, defaced, and stripped of all human dignity! That faith was rewarded instantly with eternal life!

Would you not take a cue from this thief and demonstrate such faith today?

Let me share insight on **Luke 18:18-22**—the story of the young rich ruler—with you.

> *"And a certain ruler asked him, saying, 'Good Master, what shall I do to inherit eternal life?' [19]And Jesus said unto him, 'Why callest thou me good? None is good, save one, that is, God. [20]Thou knowest the commandments, Do not commit adultery, Do not kill, Do not steal, Do not bear false witness, Honour thy father and thy mother.' [21]And he said, 'All these have I kept from my youth up.' [22]Now when Jesus heard these things, he said unto him, 'Yet lackest thou one thing: sell all that thou hast, and distribute unto the poor, and thou shalt have treasure in heaven: and come, follow me."*

Jesus told the young rich ruler, "Come follow me; that is how I can guarantee you eternal life." Do you know why Jesus asked him to follow Him? It is because Jesus is the model. If you follow Him, you can never go astray.

> *"For we have not an high priest which cannot be touched with the feeling of our infirmities; but was in all points tempted like as we are, yet without sin."( **Hebrews 4:15**)*

Jesus experienced everything that challenges humanity and yet survived them all. Following Him guarantees eternal life!

## 2. YOU WILL NOT PERISH

> *"Then Peter said, 'Lo, we have left all, and followed thee.'*
> *²⁹And he said unto them, Verily I say unto you, There is no*
> *man that hath left house, or parents, or brethren, or wife,*
> *or children, for the kingdom of God's sake, ³⁰Who shall not*
> *receive manifold more in this present time, and in the world*
> *to come life everlasting." (Luke 18:28-30)*

What Jesus is saying here is that whosoever puts Him first, by following Him, shall not only be guaranteed eternal life but will gain back much more than he has sacrificed for the sake of the kingdom of God. You will not lack provision, protection, healing, and deliverance. The Good Shepherd will nourish you both spiritually and physically. That is all guaranteed. But you have a part to play as prescribed in **Joshua 1:8**:

> *"This book of the law shall not depart out of thy mouth; but*
> *thou shalt meditate therein day and night, that thou mayest*
> *observe to do according to all that is written therein: for*
> *then thou shalt make thy way prosperous, and then thou*
> *shalt have good success."*

That part also involves what is in **2 Timothy 2:15**:

> *"Study to shew thyself approved unto God, a workman that*
> *needeth not to be ashamed, rightly dividing the word of*
> *truth."*

God requires that you spend quality time meditating on His word, internalising it, and following what it says. It is only then that you will benefit from it. Study the Bible, know it, store it in your heart, meditate on it, and let it instruct and guide your every step so that you can enjoy success! These are the things you have to do. You also need to pray without ceasing to keep the connection lines between you and God open (**1 Thessalonians 5:17**).

Your part is to 'put wood in the fire' to ensure the fire does not go out. In other words, you must remain spiritually alert and sensitive to keep hearing from Him.

*"The LORD is my shepherd; I have everything I need."*
**(Psalm 23:1, NCV)**

By following the Good Shepherd, you will not lack provision because He is your Provider. In **Psalm 37:25**, David exclaims,

*"I have been young, and now am old; yet have I not seen the righteous forsaken, nor his seed begging bread."*

Think about that! David lived for seventy years, and all through that time, he never saw the righteous forsaken! David said that he had never seen anyone who followed the Lord forsaken or their children beg for bread because food and other provisions are guaranteed when you genuinely follow the Lord.

"I have never seen" means that it has never happened before. If you are concerned with getting a job, what to eat, or anything for that matter, the solution is simple: Follow Jesus!

### 3. DIVINE PROTECTION

How is anyone going to get to you while the Good Shepherd is with you? It is impossible! They cannot get to you for Scripture says,

*"He that dwelleth in the secret place of the most High shall abide under the shadow of the Almighty. ²I will say of the Lord, He is my refuge and my fortress: my God; in him will I trust. ³Surely he shall deliver thee from the snare of the fowler, and from the noisome pestilence… ⁵Thou shalt not be afraid for the terror by night; nor for the arrow that flieth by day; ⁶Nor for the pestilence that walketh in darkness; nor for the destruction that wasteth at noonday. ⁷A thousand shall fall at thy side, and ten thousand at thy right hand; but it shall not come nigh thee. ⁸Only with thine eyes shalt thou behold and see the reward of the wicked. ⁹Because thou hast made the Lord, which is my refuge, even the most High, thy habitation; ¹⁰There shall no evil befall thee, neither shall any plague come nigh thy dwelling. ¹¹For he shall give his angels charge over thee, to keep thee in all thy ways. ¹²They shall bear thee up in their hands, lest thou dash thy foot against a stone. ¹³Thou shalt tread upon the lion and adder: the young lion and the dragon shalt thou trample*

*under feet. ¹⁴Because he hath set his love upon me, therefore will I deliver him: I will set him on high, because he hath known my name."(**Psalm 91:1-14**)*

The Good Shepherd assures you of His protection. The arrows by day will not locate you; the destruction at noonday will not be your portion; the terror of the night, the snare of the fowler, and the pestilence that walks in darkness; none of them will have a chance against you! It is incredible when you are following God!

I remember the early days of my career when I worked for a company in the Niger Delta. I was working in one of the flow stations, and then one day, as I sat down on my seat, a snake came through my window. As the snake raised its head for my neck, it froze and died there! Someone who had just walked into my office to see me saw it and screamed, "Boss, see there's a snake behind you!" And I turned to see the dead snake. What killed it, nobody could explain, but I know *the Good Shepherd* did it!

*If you are concerned about anything in life, the solution is simple: Follow Jesus!*

I also remember another time when the youth in one of our operations' host communities decided to kidnap me. They had made their plans. At the set time, while I approached a point on the road, some of them intercepted me, and I came out of the car and spoke with them. We talked, and finally, I drove off. About three days later, one of them came to my office and asked me, "Ol' boy, what do you always carry in this your pocket? We had planned to kidnap you, but instead, when we saw you, we started playing with you." He asked me to show him what was inside my pocket because he was sure that it was not only Jesus. I told him it was only Jesus and nothing else, except my car keys! Talk about divine protection! That is what Jesus guarantees!

David declares:

*"The LORD is my light and my salvation; whom shall I fear? the LORD is the strength of my life; of whom shall I be afraid? ²When the wicked, even mine enemies and my foes, came upon me to eat up my flesh, they stumbled and fell."(**Psalm 27:1-2**)*

Rock-solid assurance!

### 4. DELIVERANCE

The Bible tells of how three kings ganged up and came against King Jehoshaphat. And the Lord told Jehoshaphat that he did not need to engage them in a battle to obtain victory. The moment he heard that he did not need to fight, the king did something unusual. He called the singers with instruments to start singing and praising God, thus relegating the soldiers to the rear.

In today's world, it will be like having battle-ready people around you with their machine guns, but you decide to pick up a musical instrument to start playing in their midst! The man with a machine gun is aiming at you, but you are dancing. They will think that one was mad. It is only people who are *following* God and have heard from Him who can do such. Only people led by Him like 'zombies' can act upon an instruction like that; people who will ignore the heavy military might and presence of the enemy but start dancing and praising God. Jehoshaphat did that, and God Himself summarily dismissed the war! That is how you are guaranteed deliverance. (**2 Chronicles 20:1-30**)

In **Acts 27:22-23, 31**, Apostle Paul and others were involved in a ship disaster, and his co-travellers were trying to jump out of the ship, but he told them to stop that course of action. He said to them, "An angel stood by me this night and told me that no man should perish on this trip." And I declare that you can rest assured that as you embark on a journey which the Good Shepherd has directed you to embark upon, no one travelling with you shall perish in the name of Jesus!

Paul assured them that no one would die provided they stayed on the ship because of what the angel of God told him the night before. They heeded the condition, and none was lost! That is divine deliverance. Many of us run from pillar to post, even when God says, "Be still!" Unfortunately, people look at the circumstance and start running instead of heeding what God is saying!

About the time I was planning to get married, I was on a plane to Port Harcourt one day with my fiancée (now, my wife) when suddenly, we ran into horrible weather, and all on board were sensing trouble. The plane had lost altitude. Fear came upon everyone, and people began to cry. I saw one Alhaji there who was crying. There was also a woman who had on expensive-looking jewellery around her neck; by looking at her, you could tell that she was well-to-do—she too was crying profusely. But while all this was going on, God had spoken to me that I would get married. Of course, that meant I could not be in a plane crash. Each time the plane rocked from one side to another, my wife would scream, "*Jesus!*" I tried to calm her down, but the other passengers would say, "*Let her pray!*"

Today, I look back at that incident and smile because one could see by the level of fear demonstrated on that plane that day that people do not want to die at all! By the time we landed, you needed to have seen people on board crying—lots of people were dishevelled! Our co-travellers testified that they observed that each time my wife shouted, "*Jesus!*" the turbulence subsided! That was why they bellowed at me to let her pray! Of course, I could not help wondering why the other passengers on board could not pray themselves!

All that time, I held on to God's voice which told me that I would get married. It was clear and reassuring enough because if God said I would get married, then I knew I was going to make it regardless of the weather and turbulence. Nobody could stop me.

That same God is telling you that you will reach your destination! Nothing can change that because you are unstoppable when the Good Shepherd leads you! Therefore, every spiritual watchdog positioned around you to confuse your path stands paralyzed henceforth! You will arise and shine! Men and women will come to the brightness of your rising from this moment forward, in the name of Jesus Christ that died and rose again!

### 5. HEALING

Today, many people visit false prophets, who tell them to go and bathe in certain rivers 'to be healed', in a bid to imitate the miracle of Naaman in the Bible. But this is so wrong as there can be no help from any source apart from God—the Good Shepherd! When Elisha told Naaman, the commander of the army of the king of Aram, to go bathe in River Jordan for his healing from leprosy, his response was, "Are there no better rivers in Samaria?" He probably thought in his heart when responding to prophet Elisha: "What is this man saying? I told him I am sick, and he is asking me to go and bathe in the dirty Jordan? How is that going to solve my problem?" Let us consider what Naaman said:

> *11"But Naaman was wroth, and went away, and said, 'Behold, I thought, He will surely come out to me, and stand, and call on the name of the Lord his God, and strike his hand over the place, and recover the leper. 12Are not Abana and Pharpar, rivers of Damascus, better than all the waters of Israel? May I not wash in them, and be clean?' So he turned and went away in a rage."* (**2 Kings 5:11-12**)

At the onset, Naaman did not *follow* the counsel given him by the prophet. But when he *obeyed* the prophet's instruction, he reaped the blessing of obedience—God healed him! The key here is **obedience!** I shared earlier about what God told me when my son was hospitalized with pneumonia—"*Go thy way, thy son liveth!*" Note that He did not say I should go and fast for twenty days or anything like that: He just said, "*Go thy way!*" and He did not lie. I went my way, and my son lived! That is God! When you *follow* Him by obeying simple instructions, your healing is guaranteed.

Once I was scheduled to undergo surgery abroad. After doing all the pre-surgery tests, I was programmed for surgery the following day. But before then, I had committed the surgical operation to God in prayer, for God's will to be done. As I slept that night, God showed me a vision of me involved in an accident. I asked Him if it could be stopped, and He told me that the surgery was going to be a disaster. When I woke up, I called the doctor and told him I was not coming in for the surgery. I said, "It is over!" He responded that he did not understand my message. I sent him a mail informing him that he would not understand because my decision was spiritual. I went on to let him know that I had spoken with God, and He said, "*No surgery!*"

Doctors do not decide anything; God does! When God said, "*No surgery!*" for me, that was final! I testify to you today that I am still standing—there was no surgery! Hallelujah!

The key is knowing how to hear from God—which is crucial in following the Good Shepherd.

### 6. ABUNDANCE

The Bible tells us how Isaac tried to relocate from Gerar, where he was sojourning (**Genesis 26:1-13**). God told him not to relocate but to stay in Gerar. Gerar was a barren land because there was a famine, yet God told Isaac to remain there.

To fully understand how difficult that instruction was, we should remember that their mainstay was farming. Since a famine persisted in the land, productivity was zero because anything you planted could not grow.

*For your abundance and breakthrough to genuinely manifest, you must listen to and obey God!*

Isaac saw that there was famine where he was and sought to run away to greener pastures. But God said to him, *"Stay and plant where you are!"* The Bible records that Isaac sowed in that land. You need to understand that sowing during a famine is challenging because the ground has nothing. But when God has said, *"Sow!"*; sow, you must! Isaac had to follow God's leading and put the seed into the ground, irrespective of his personal feelings about it. And look at the result that sprang from this hardcore obedience! In the same year, Isaac reaped a hundred-fold, and he grew and became very prosperous! All of that during a famine!

Now, you might not get the full picture of the level of abundance that Isaac got into by *following* in a time of famine if you do not understand what Jesus was saying about levels of yields in **Mark 4**. Jesus was talking about sowing seeds on different grounds. He said that the highest yield obtainable when you plant in a fertile land is a hundred-fold:

> *"And some fell on good ground, and did yield fruit that sprang up and increased; and brought forth, some thirty, and some sixty, and some an hundred." (***Mark 4:8***)*

The Bible says, if you sow on good ground, you will get returns in the order of thirty, sixty, and hundred-fold, which meant that Isaac got the maximum yield possible of a good (fertile) ground from a barren land because he followed God's instructions! God asked him to stay, and he obeyed! In the same vein, for your abundance and breakthrough to genuinely manifest, you must listen to and obey God!

Obedience to the voice of God is the reason someone selling ground-nuts can be flying all over the world. In contrast to someone else who is supposedly into a more significant business, like a car dealer who has nothing to show for it! It is all because

> *"it is not of him that willeth, nor he that runneth, but of God that showeth mercy."* (**Romans 9:16**)

The point is that God can bless you just as He has blessed others in very mysterious ways. We should never try to reason out God's instructions with our finite minds or foot-drag when He has given the command.

There are restaurants overseas where you cannot eat unless you have booked a seat some three or even six months in advance. Why so? Because the chef operating that restaurant is a "celebrity chef!"

Now, if you want to study catering, some people would probably say, "Why not Engineering or some other 'big-name' course? Why catering?" But the reality is that many engineers have no money. But here is a chef who has hundreds of customers booking months in advance to eat in a restaurant, and the celebrity chef is earning almost thirty thousand pounds every day, net of all expenses! I am trying to point out that you should trust God to decide what you would do in life. Solomon said,

> *Whatsoever thy hand findeth to do, do it with thy might; for there is no work, nor device, nor knowledge, nor wisdom, in the grave, whither thou goest. I returned, and saw under the sun, that the race is not to the swift, nor the battle to the strong, neither yet bread to the wise, nor yet riches to men of understanding, nor yet favour to men of skill; but time and chance happeneth to them all.* (**Ecclesiastes 9:10-11**)

Whatsoever God asks you to do, do it with all your might; for therein lies your success!

### 7.  NO ONE WILL EVER PLUCK YOU OUT OF HIS HAND

When you follow the Good Shepherd, no one can pluck you out of His hand. The Bible says,

> *"Your life is hid with Christ in God"* (**Colossians 3:3**)

That is why Jesus said,

*". . . neither shall any man pluck them out of my hand . . . and no man is able to pluck them out of my Father's hand."(John 10:28-29)*

Following Him means that a wall of fire surrounds you through which no one can reach you. When you are following Jesus, no man can pluck you from His hand. Conversely, when you stop following Jesus, it becomes a calamity.

*When you are following Jesus, no man can pluck you from His hand.*

King Saul stopped following God, and when he did, the Spirit of God left him—what a calamity! The Bible says that an evil spirit entered him, and king Saul lost his way in life! And worse was yet to come. Before his disobedience, the Bible tells us how king Saul drove away all the witches and sorcerers in Israel. But when he went astray, the same man went secretly to consult with a witch—the witch of Endor. He sought to know whether Israel would win the war at hand from a witch!

How terrible it is to know God and then replace Him with what He despises—such was the case of King Saul. He left God and followed a witch, someone with a familiar spirit; an abomination before God! How terrible!

Unfortunately, many of those of the household of God today, supposedly 'serving Him' and claiming to be born again, are quick to run to a native doctor or a spiritualist when problems arise. How sad! God can solve any problem, and He will solve yours, but you must remain in Him!

The temptation that you cannot bear will not come to you, and God will make a way of escape when temptation does come (**1 Corinthians 10:13**). Because some people think that they are not getting answers to their prayers quickly, they start seeking alternatives.

You have to drop that mentality and rest assured that God will answer your prayers. He will hasten His word to perform it in your life. You will not have to go anywhere else apart from God. All you need to do is to *follow Him*!

The scriptures document several examples of people who stopped following God. Demas is one of them (**2 Timothy 4:10**), and Judas Iscariot

**The Good Shepherd**

is perhaps the most notable one. Judas Iscariot was a close associate of Jesus—an apostle—yet he stopped following Him. Jesus remarked that Judas Iscariot was,

*"... [a] son of perdition." (**John 17:12**)*

That will not be your story in the name of Jesus. You will not be a castaway!

# CONCLUSION

When you read about Abraham's experience with God; and other Bible characters, including contemporary believers, on following God's leading, their stories often sound amazing. But note that following God is a pretty complicated road to travel when you are in the flesh!

The Good Shepherd's options for the sheep do not always make sense to the natural—carnal—man. But to qualify for the blessing of *following* the Good Shepherd, the sheep must accept and follow the Good Shepherd's counsel, always! You need to understand this point in your walk with God so that you do not shut down His voice, thinking or saying that the devil is speaking, just because a particular word from God sounds strange or too difficult for you to accept. His ways are not your ways. And they are not always easy from the perspective of the flesh (**Romans 8:5-8**).

By the time we get to the section on *hearing His voice*—the hearing dimension—your eyes shall be enlightened, and your understanding will know when the Good Shepherd is speaking, regardless of 'the strangeness' of His instruction.

# Chapter 6

**The Good Shepherd**

# The Trusting Dimension

*'Tis so sweet to trust in Jesus,*
*and to take him at his word;*
*just to rest upon his promise,*
*and to know, "Thus saith the Lord."*

*The first stanza of "'Tis so sweet to trust in Jesus" (1882)*

*by Louisa M. R. Stead, 1850 -1917*

*"Thou preparest a table before me in the presence of mine enemies: thou anointest my head with oil; my cup runneth over." (Psalm 23:5)*

**N**ow, let us take a more in-depth look at the fifth verse of the twenty-third Psalm. One thing stands out in the sheep's relationship with the Shepherd: they trust Him completely! If they did not trust the Shepherd, then there is no way that they would have been able to eat at a table prepared by Him and set up amid the enemy. No way! Would you be able to sit and peacefully eat if it were you? You must trust the person enough to be able to eat in that setting. But the sheep do not care once the Shepherd is there. They are carefree in His presence. Nothing matters to them in that environment because they know that the Shepherd can take care of all the issues that may arise. That is where Christ wants you to be today—ever trusting and confident in His love.

Let us examine an incident between Peter and Jesus in scripture.

*"And in the fourth watch of the night Jesus went unto them, walking on the sea. ²⁶And when the disciples saw him walking on the sea, they were troubled, saying, It is a spirit; and they cried out for fear. ²⁷But straightway Jesus spake unto them, saying, Be of good cheer; it is I; be not afraid. ²⁸And Peter answered him and said, Lord, if it be thou, bid me come unto thee on the water. ²⁹And he said, Come. And when Peter was come down out of the ship, he walked on the water, to go to Jesus. ³⁰But when he saw the wind boisterous, he was afraid; and beginning to sink, he cried, saying, Lord, save me. ³¹And immediately Jesus stretched forth his hand, and caught him, and said unto him, O thou of little faith, wherefore didst thou doubt?" (Matthew 14:25-31)*

Jesus said to Peter, *"Come!"* and Peter responded without a thought—that is how sheep responds to their shepherd. Peter's response was without any hesitation whatsoever! Of course, Peter had never seen a man walk on water before, yet he did not give it a thought; if he had, he most likely would not have taken one step into the water! Hence the Bible says:

**The Good Shepherd**

> *"Trust in the LORD with all thine heart; and lean not unto thine own understanding. ⁶In all thy ways acknowledge him, and he shall direct thy paths." (**Proverbs 3:5-6**)*

Peter stepped into the water! A human being's mental state dictates that by natural laws, a man stepping on to water is an anchor—the moment that person gets into the water, they would sink! Therefore, in following God, you should not waste time reasoning. If Jesus says, *"Come!"* then, you go! And so, Peter was doing well walking on water until he shifted his gaze to the boisterous waves, which then introduced fear into him, and he doubted.

Jesus read the situation well and afterwards rebuked him, *"Peter, why did you doubt?"* In other words, *"Why did you stop trusting me? Why did you shift your attention away from me? You were doing okay until you doubted!"* Thus, we need to understand what it means to trust someone.

# WHAT DOES IT MEAN TO TRUST?

### 1. TO TRUST IS TO HAVE CONFIDENCE IN THE ABILITY, INTEGRITY, STRENGTH, AND POWER OF SOMEONE

#### *TRUSTING IN HIS ABILITY*

Like sheep trust their shepherd's capacity to provide for their need, you must trust that God can do much more than we can ask or even think (**Ephesians 3:20**).

> *"For with God nothing shall be impossible" (**Luke 1:37**)*

God also proved His ability when He said,

> *"Behold, I am the LORD, the God of all flesh: is there anything too hard for me?" (**Jeremiah 32:27**)*

The sheep trust the ability of the Good Shepherd. They know that no wolf can take them from His hands. The Bible tells us about the sensational story of Shadrach, Meshach, and Abednego in **Daniel 3:1-30**. In *v. 16 & 17*, when they spoke to the king, they said:

---

> *"...We are not careful to answer thee in this matter. [17]If it be so, our God whom we serve is able to deliver us from the burning fiery furnace, and he will deliver us out of thine hand, O king."*

What they were saying is, "We do not know the way it is going to work, but we still trust His judgment. If His judgement is that we must die on this occasion, then it is fine!" That is total trust in God. Paul echoed this thought when he wrote,

> *"To live is Christ and to die is gain." (**Philippians 1:21**)*

No one else but Jesus!

### TRUSTING HIS INTEGRITY

**Numbers 23:19** captures the essence of what it means to trust the integrity of God:

> *"God is not a man, that he should lie; neither the son of man, that he should repent: hath he said, and shall he not do it? or hath he spoken, and shall he not make it good?" (**Numbers 23:19**)*

That is the God we serve; when He says something, He performs it!

### TRUSTING IN HIS STRENGTH

Hear what God is saying to you:

> *"Hast thou not known? hast thou not heard, that the everlasting God, the LORD, the Creator of the ends of the earth, fainteth not, neither is weary? there is no searching of his understanding."( **Isaiah 40:28**)*

God is speaking about Himself as One who lasts forever. His strength does not diminish. Even though everybody gets tired, God never gets tired. If you depend on a man, he will disappoint you when he gets tired, but God is never exhausted. His strength is everlasting!

When Mohammed Ali boxed, he wore shorts with the name and logo of the 'Everlast' brand embossed in the front of the waistband. Of course, as the name implies, you could see Ali portray that he had this kind of strength that lasts forever. That was an inferior and inadequate comparison with God's strength because wherever you see 'everlast', you cannot but think of the everlasting God. But then, we know that however strong a man or product may be, it can never last forever like God! He is the Everlasting One whose strength never diminishes. That is why the Bible says:

> *"They that wait upon the LORD shall renew their strength;*
> *they shall mount up with wings as eagles; they shall run,*
> *and not be weary; and they shall walk, and not faint."* (**Isaiah 40:31**)

The old and the young get tired, but God never tires. He is laden with strength. The Bible says,

> *"If thou faint in the day of adversity your strength is*
> *small."* (**Proverbs 24:10**)

Man's strength is tiny in comparison to God's energy which is infinite! David boasts of Him thus:

> *"The LORD is my light and my salvation; whom shall I*
> *fear? the LORD is the strength of my life; of whom shall I*
> *be afraid?"* (**Psalm 27:1**)

When you trust someone, you are trusting also in his strength. If wolves were to show up this moment, you could say this man is not a weakling; he will deal with them.

### *TRUSTING IN HIS POWER*

To trust in the Good Shepherd means to trust in His power.

> *"God hath spoken once; twice have I heard this; that power*
> *belongeth unto God."* (**Psalm 62:11**)

Power belongs to God and God alone!

Having full confidence in God's ability, strength, integrity, and power is what it means to trust in Him! Your faith is not only in God's attributes but, more importantly, you trust Him.

---

## 2. TO TRUST IS TO DEPEND ON SOMEONE ELSE

> *"Trust in the LORD with all thine heart; and lean not unto thine own understanding. [6] In all thy ways acknowledge him, and he shall direct thy paths."* (**Proverbs 3:5-6**)

To trust God is to rely on Him entirely, knowing that He cannot disappoint nor fail you. It is to take God at His word.

In **Luke 5:1-11**, we see Peter, a super fisherman who supposedly knew everything about fishing, had fished all day and caught nothing. But when Jesus came on the scene, He said to him, *"Now launch out!"* And Peter said, "See, I have done everything I know as a professional fisherman today, nevertheless at Your word, I will launch again." In other words, Peter was inadvertently saying to Jesus, "I trust you."

Someone may say to you, "Have you been to such and such office?" And you may respond, "Oh, I have been there, but there was nothing!" but then, you are told, by the revelation of the Holy Spirt, "Go back there!"; would you go? Won't you feel like they are wasting your time? You may even whine about how all your attempts met with frustration, but the question is, "Do you trust Jesus? It is He asking you to go back there!" The truth is that the person speaking is not speaking his own words; he is echoing what God is saying—*"Thus says the Lord …!"*

> *"...Believe in the LORD your God, so shall ye be established; believe his prophets, so shall ye prosper."* (**2 Chronicles 20:20**)

That is what the Bible says—*believe in the Word!* Hence, Peter also said, "… at Your word; I am doing this because You say so, Jesus." The point is that the sheep trust the Good Shepherd, and whenever He speaks, they believe and obey Him.

## 3. TO TRUST IS TO BELIEVE IN THE FAITHFULNESS OF SOMEONE

To trust a person is to consider that person trustworthy, and when trouble comes, he will not abandon you. God says:

> *"When thou passest through the waters, I will be with thee; and through the rivers, they shall not overflow thee: when thou walkest through the fire, thou shalt not be burned;*

*neither shall the flame kindle upon thee." (Isaiah 43:2)*

God assures you that He will be there with you when you go through thick and thin. He does not cut and run when things get tough and rough. He is there with you in the thick of it. That is why you need to hold on to Him. You need to trust Him completely and absolutely!

The Good Shepherd will never disappoint His sheep. He is Jehovah Jireh, the Lord, our Provider. Isaac said to Abraham, his father: "I can see the wood for the fire, but where is the lamb?" His trusting father replied,

> *"My son, God will provide himself a lamb for a burnt offering" (Genesis 22:8)*

They got to the place appointed, and there was no ram for the sacrifice, but the Lord Himself showed up, as he will in every situation that concerns you in Jesus' name (**Genesis 22:1-14**).

In 2011, I travelled to the U. S. for an executive programme. Two and a half weeks into the programme, I had a headache and assumed it to be malaria. Now, to get malaria drugs or treatment in America can be a problem. So, I went to the hospital to treat malaria—one of the best in the area. When I got there, the first sign of trouble was when it was difficult getting someone who could analyze the ailment. As it turned out, it was not even malaria! Things got complicated from that point on, and everything unravelled quickly.

Before I knew what was happening, I was on admission, and a machine was attached to me to monitor my vital signs. The readings showed that my blood pressure was about typical (130/85). Suddenly, and without warning, my blood pressure dropped to about 80/50! Then there was a frenzy; the hospital administrators brought in several doctors and wheeled me into the intensive care unit (ICU).

When I realised what was going on, I started praying in tongues. Some of the doctors were concerned, thinking that I was going off, speaking gibberish, but one of them who understood what I was doing told them I was praying.

In my prayer, I said, "Jesus, you have never failed me before. In this place, the brethren are not with me. Prayer warriors are not here, but you are, and because you are here, I am coming out of this situation." I was consistently praying on the bed.

Finally, the doctors reported that they could not place a finger on what was wrong but that it appeared that my liver, heart and many other organs had failed. They had all kinds of lists. At that point, I smiled because I had already heard from God. They told me that they conducted a series of tests and that every single one of the tests suggested that I was okay. The question in the air then was: what happened? How would I explain to American doctors about 'spiritual *arrows?*'—they would not understand any of that. Anyhow, it did not matter what had happened; what matters is that Jesus delivers, even from unexpectedly shot arrows! He is reliable, dependable, and He is Lord, and therefore, can be trusted. Hallelujah!

Even when there are no prayer warriors or pastors around, Jesus is always there! He said,

> *"I will never leave you nor forsake you." (**Hebrews 13:5, NKJV**)*

And you can bank on that because He is reliable. He does not need help to get you out of danger; He is all-sufficient! He never disappoints as humans do. If a wolf is coming and the Shepherd is going with the sheep, you can rest assured that He will stay and defend the sheep from the wolf. He will never run away. He will face the wolf squarely. He has said and still says,

> *"I will be an enemy unto thine enemies, and an adversary unto thine adversaries." (**Exodus 23:22**)*

He will face them on your behalf. He is that faithful.

In **Esther 4:16**, Queen Esther was confronted with a problem and had to go before the king. She was caught in a dilemma because one could not approach the king uninvited according to the law—should you go in to see him and he is not favourably disposed to you, that could result in the king ordering his guards to chop off your head! So, Esther said to her people, "I am going in uninvited, start praying! If I perish, I perish!" But she never perished because the One that she trusted granted her favour.

Similarly, the Bible also tells us about Shadrach, Meshach, and Abednego, who defied King Nebuchadnezzar's order because it was at variance with their faith. They answered the king,

*"... we are not careful to answer thee in this matter. If it be so, our God whom we serve is able to deliver us from the burning fiery furnace, and he will deliver us out of thine hand, O king. (**Daniel 3:16-17**)*

*There is a glory to be revealed!*

Nothing happened after they said those words—no noise; they said nothing else. They were rock steady—no shaking anywhere. Everything to them was as normal as ever. Their defiance made the King fume with rage, and he ordered increasing the fire's intensity seven times. In other words, if the initial temperature was 100 degrees Celsius, they made it 700 degrees Celsius! The king wanted to roast them alive that bad! The heat that emanated from the fire was so intense; the flames devoured the soldiers who threw the young men into the fire.

Imagine such a situation with some of today's Christians! You can bet many would have been looking around in trepidation and whispering to themselves, "God should have shown up by now, don't you think? Are you sure we did not make a mistake?" They would have started fidgeting, saying, "Ol' boy, are you sure we would be alright? Maybe it is time to go back and bow as commanded. We have been saying, 'Jesus! Jesus!' but can you see the level of the fiery furnace?" But not Shadrach, Meshach, and Abednego! They stood their ground and remained resolute in their decision to defy the king's order. Eventually, the king's guards threw them into the fiery furnace.

To comprehend the level of trust demonstrated by these three men, one needs to understand that all that time, God did not show up to rescue them until after they had been tossed into the fiery furnace. Yet, their belief in Him did not wane for one moment! Think about that!

That is what sometimes happens when you are standing for Jesus—the problem could even worsen to test your faith. From a hundred degrees to seven hundred degrees, and then it gets more challenging! But I tell you, there is a glory to be revealed. The Bible says that this present time's suffering is nothing compared to the glory that shall be revealed in us (**Romans 8:18**). Brethren, there is a glory to be revealed!

Now, after the strong men threw Shadrach, Meshach, and Abednego into the fire, something happened—the Good Shepherd was already waiting for them in the fire! He did not go in there to join them; He was waiting for them in the fiery furnace! Think about that.

The king looked and screamed, "There's a fourth person in the fire!" Jesus was waiting for them because His word had already assured them that He would never leave them nor forsake them. You can read the full story in **Daniel 3:1-30**.

As a child of God, you need to know and understand that there are some things you will see or experience in life which you will not be able to explain, but you can trust the Good Shepherd to see you through because He is reliable. If you follow the news and what is happening around the world, you will be nonplused. As human beings, we do not always get the whole perspective on issues. There are questions to which we will only get the answers when we see God. That is why the Bible says that,

> *"The secret things belong unto the LORD our God: but those things which are revealed belong unto us and to our children forever." (**Deuteronomy 29:29**)*

Jesus can be trusted. If you must trust anyone, it has to be Him!

He never disappointed Daniel when he was in the den of lions—he came out unscathed (**Daniel 6:1-24**). The lions *sowed* 'not eating Daniel' and reaped an abundant harvest of flesh later on! When they later brought all the enemies of Daniel together with their wives and children, the lions had a field day. That was how the Good Shepherd delivered Daniel!

He never disappointed Mary and Martha. The day He went to their house, Mary sat at His feet, paying rapt attention to what He was teaching. On the other hand, Martha was running around, caught up in the activity of being a great host. And Jesus told her, "Martha, you are careful about too many things. There is something essential, and Mary has sat down to get this thing." That is how close He was to them. He loved them and visited their home. Then something terrible happened; Lazarus, their brother, fell ill and died! While faced with this challenge, Jesus was far away and could not intervene when it mattered most—or so they thought.

When Jesus finally showed up, they said, "If You had been here earlier, our brother would not have died." But they were wrong. Jesus told them that He—who was standing right there in their midst—is the Resurrection and the Life! They did not have to wait till the Last Day; Lazarus, their brother, would be raised from the dead that day! If He wants someone to arise from the dead, that is what would happen. He was asking them to trust Him. (**John 11:1-45**)

Jesus can make a way where there is no way. He can put rivers in the desert. He took a multitude across the Red Sea, where there was no way. Ever imagined what it would take to build a bridge across the Red Sea? You would have to construct a 190-mile bridge! A task that would have taken a considerable chunk of their resources, yet God did it for free!

There is no limit to what God can do. What is more, He gave His life for His sheep as the ultimate price of His commitment to saving them. He loves His sheep dearly and has invested so much in them. That is why you should trust Him.

# EVERYONE ELSE IS A HIRELING

You need to know that Jesus is not a hireling. Our parents gave birth to us, yet in comparison to the Good Shepherd, they are hirelings! Apart from Jesus, everyone else is a hireling and will disappoint you. They will run when they see the wolves coming for you. Do not be deceived.

I relate here the true story of a man: his younger brother lived with him in his "boy's quarters"—a back house usually reserved for servants of the well-to-do. One day, armed robbers went to his house and had a hard time trying to get in because he had this heavy security door that needed sophisticated equipment to break down than what the robbers had. So, the robbers resorted to using the man's younger brother as bait. They informed him that if he did not open the door to them, they would shoot his sibling. At that point, the younger brother told them point-blank that the man they were baiting was very selfish and would not budge, even if they killed him. Sensing that the younger brother was right, they gave up on their plans and left empty-handed. That older brother was a hireling. When wolves attack, the hireling flees and does not care what happens to the sheep!

All the boastings and feigned display of confidence in people who say, "He is my brother, or she is my sister" is transient. I am not advocating that you have no regard for relationships—filial or otherwise—but I am saying that the hard truth is that you cannot trust any human being! The arm of flesh will fail you. You cannot trust in horses and chariots. Some people have guns in their houses, but what is that in the face of imminent danger?

*Jacob stole Esau's birthright—and they were twins! Judas Iscariot betrayed Jesus to His assailants! Your spouse can disappoint you! Only the Good Shepherd is truly trustworthy!*

A friend of mine testified of how about twenty armed robbers came to his house. He and his family were upstairs, in trepidation! The *maiguard* (the local security guard), who hid nearby when the robbers gained entrance into the premises, heard one of the robbers say, "Are you sure someone is living in this house?" Another remarked, "See cobwebs everywhere! Certainly, nobody has lived here for a long time!" And yet another robber asked, "Are you sure you got the right address?" They began arguing among themselves and concluded that no one had lived there for a long time because of the thick cobwebs at the front door. So, they turned around and left! The *maiguard* overheard their conversation.

After the armed robbers left, the *maiguard* came out from hiding and started looking for the said cobwebs—lo and behold, there was nothing like that on the door! Yet, God made the robbers see cobwebs, and that sent them away! There were no cobwebs, but God made them see cobwebs! Horses and chariots and security guards will fail you, but Jesus has His unconventional arsenal. Trust Him!

Someone may say, "I trust my brother", but remember that Jacob stole Esau's birthright—and they were twins! Friends can disappoint you. Judas Iscariot betrayed Jesus to His assailants!

Your spouse can disappoint you—consider Abraham and Sarah. Whenever Abraham sensed he would get into trouble on account of Sarah's beauty, he would tell her, "Please say you are my sister so that they don't kill me because of you!" It did not matter to Abraham that they could have slept with his wife! The same thing happened with Isaac, Abraham's son, and Rebecca, his wife! Many would say, "I trust my wife!" But they forget that it was Delilah—a woman Samson loved dearly—who revealed his secret to his enemies so that they could capture and destroy him!

Others trust their children, but they forget what Absalom did to David, his father, in **2 Samuel 15:1-20**.

Some trust their parents, but the Psalmist said,

> *"When my father and my mother forsake me, then the LORD will take me up."* (**Psalm 27:10**)

You need to understand that even your parents can forsake you, else the Psalmist would not have said, *'when'*; he could have said *'if'*! God is the only Father you can trust.

The story of Jephthah in **Judges 11:30-40** is very instructive here. We see how Jephthah made a vow to God that if He helped him to be victorious in battle, he would present as a sacrifice the first thing that comes out of his house to welcome him when he returned home! Sadly, his daughter and the only child ran out of the house to welcome him home from the battle. Imagine that! Why did Jephthah not offer himself as a sacrifice to God when making the vow?

# TRUST THE GOOD SHEPHERD AT ALL TIMES

As sheep trust their shepherd totally and absolutely, so must we, the Lord—our Shepherd. Sheep, never look back. They do not run to another when the heat is on. Instead, they move closer to the shepherd. When there is a problem, they do not run here and there seeking help from other shepherds. They hurdle closer to their shepherd. That is why the sheep are always healthy—they are not worried. The Bible says:

> *"Be careful for nothing; but in everything by prayer and supplication with thanksgiving let your requests be made known unto God."* (**Philippians 4:6**)

You do not have to carry your problems all by yourself—you have the Good Shepherd to do that! In **Matthew 6:25-34**, Jesus said that He feeds the lilies even though they are of less value to Him in comparison to you. Now, if He does that for grass, why should His people be anxious?

Sheep never fret; they depend on the shepherd. They trust him for everything.

When David confronted Goliath saying, "I will give your flesh unto the fowls of the air, and to the beasts of the field", he was speaking from his experience as a shepherd, knowing that his Shepherd would take care of the Goliath problem! People were concerned for David, even though none tried to stop him from going up against a well-trained giant! Instead, they brought the weapons and armour of king Saul and put them on David, but the young lad said to them, "Sirs, I have not proven these. Please take them off me!"

David was saying in effect, "As a shepherd, I know better to trust my Shepherd." He recounted how, while shepherding, a lion came for his sheep and by the strength of God his Shepherd, he took out the lion. At another time, a bear attacked the sheep, and by the power of God, his Shepherd, he was able to slay the bear also!

Therefore, he concluded that that same God would deliver the Goliath of Gath, the uncircumcised Philistine, into his hand! (**1 Samuel 17:1-51**). "David must be out of his mind", they thought, but the Good Shepherd came through for the lad!

That same God, the One who keeps you alive and makes you overcome the afflictions and troubles of life, has not changed. Trust Him!

# Chapter 7

**The Good Shepherd**

# The Knowledge Dimension

*More about Jesus let me learn,*

*More of His holy will discern;*

*Spirit of God my teacher be,*

*Showing the things of Christ to me.*

*"More about Jesus would I know" (1887)*

*by Eliza Edmunds Hewitt, 1851-1920*

*"I am the good shepherd, and know my sheep, and am known of mine." (**John 10:14**)*

In this verse of Scripture, Jesus shares what constitutes the core of the relationship between the sheep and the Shepherd—that is, *the knowledge dimension*. He says, *"I know my sheep and my sheep know me."* The sheep must know the Shepherd. If you do not know the Shepherd as sheep, then you can be deceived and may suddenly start following someone else, just because you cannot discern. For example, you can go into a church meeting where the pastor is not serving God as his Master (obviously not a sheep of the Good Shepherd!) and end up staying there for several years without discernment! And then you will be deceived! That is why your knowledge of the Good Shepherd is crucial.

*"Even so every good tree bringeth forth good fruit; but a corrupt tree bringeth forth evil fruit." (**Matthew 7:15**)*

Several people have come claiming to be Jesus. At least, I know the one that was called *"Jesu Oyingbo"*. He has been dead a long time now! Therefore, you have the responsibility of knowing the true Shepherd. If you do not know the Good Shepherd as a priority, false shepherds will mislead you to follow Satan. You have to identify His characteristics, as discussed in Part One of this book. And one of the most remarkable attributes of the Good Shepherd is that He is holy! Jesus cannot sin! If you find yourself following someone leading you into sin, you should know that such a 'shepherd' is from the pit of hell!

*"For we have not a high priest which cannot be touched with the feeling of our infirmities; but was in all points tempted like as we are, yet without sin." (**Hebrews 4:15**)*

Holiness is the most significant and distinguishing attribute of the Good Shepherd.

*"But unto the Son he saith, Thy throne, O God, is for ever and ever: a sceptre of righteousness is the sceptre of thy kingdom." (**Hebrews 1:8**)*

# UNDERSTANDING THE KNOWLEDGE CHAIN

What then does it mean to know the Shepherd? It means to have adequate information about the Shepherd or have full knowledge of Who He is. And the only way to accomplish this is to be close to Him. You should cultivate an intimate relationship with Him.

Understand this: *knowledge starts with information*. When someone mentions the word *knowledge*, what usually comes after, is the word *"understanding"* or *"revelation"*—a divine form of information. There is a knowledge chain, and it begins with information, which is what you read or hear about someone or something or what you learn through revelation.

*If you find yourself following someone leading you into sin, you should know that such a 'shepherd' is from the pit of hell!*

Believers and Unbelievers alike read the Bible, and they get information about God. But sometimes, they lack an understanding of the information they have received. But when you read with understanding, it is called *comprehension*. In other words, you read and understand or comprehend. And the application of the knowledge derived is wisdom, also known as applied knowledge. Therefore, *"to know"* is to have information (or revelation), then understand and comprehend what that information is, and correctly use such knowledge to achieve the desired end. Sometimes, *knowledge* can be a *revelation* given to you by the Spirit of God, not from books, and it does not contradict the Bible.

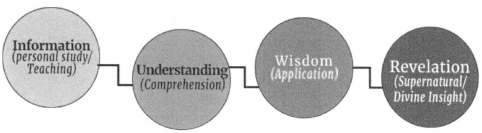

*Figure 1: The Knowledge Chain*

To know the Good Shepherd, therefore, you must have information about Him. You must understand and comprehend that information. Then, you must apply the knowledge of what you have garnered about Him in your everyday living.

# DEEPER LEVELS OF KNOWLEDGE

When we speak of knowledge, our reference is the knowledge of God. And a Christian must know God. Apostle Paul did not take this for granted in his ministry and personal walk with the Good Shepherd. He considered the knowledge of Christ to be of utmost importance in his life. In **Philippians 3:1-11**, Paul gave us essential information that suggests that this was crucial for him.

> *"Finally, my brethren, rejoice in the Lord. To write the same things to you, to me indeed is not grievous, but for you it is safe. ²] Beware of dogs, beware of evil workers, beware of the concision. ³For we are the circumcision, which worship God in the spirit, and rejoice in Christ Jesus, and have no confidence in the flesh. ⁴Though I might also have confidence in the flesh. If any other man thinketh that he hath whereof he might trust in the flesh, I more: ⁵Circumcised the eighth day, of the stock of Israel, of the tribe of Benjamin, an Hebrew of the Hebrews; as touching the law, a Pharisee; ⁶Concerning zeal, persecuting the church; touching the righteousness which is in the law, blameless. ⁷But what things were gain to me, those I counted loss for Christ. ⁸Yea doubtless, and I count all things but loss for the excellency of the knowledge of Christ Jesus my Lord: for whom I have suffered the loss of all things, and do count them but dung, that I may win Christ, ⁹And be found in him, not having mine own righteousness, which is of the law, but that which is through the faith of Christ, the righteousness which is of God by faith: ¹⁰That I may know him, and the power of his resurrection, and the fellowship of his sufferings, being made conformable unto his death; ¹¹If by any means I might attain unto the resurrection of the dead. ¹²Not as though I had already attained, either were already perfect: but I follow after, if*

*that I may apprehend that for which also I am apprehended of Christ Jesus. ¹³Brethren, I count not myself to have apprehended: but this one thing I do, forgetting those things which are behind, and reaching forth unto those things which are before, ¹⁴I press toward the mark for the prize of the high calling of God in Christ Jesus."*

In *v. 10*, the Apostle brings everything home when he says,

*"That I may know Him!"*

The knowledge of the Good Shepherd is the crux of the matter: like sheep, you must know the Good Shepherd!

It would be best if you appreciated from where Paul was coming. In **Acts 9:5**, after Jesus had intercepted him, he asked Jesus, "Who art thou?" Here was a man on his way to Damascus to arrest, prosecute, and execute Christians. Suddenly, a bright light appeared from heaven and blinded him, knocking him to the ground! Then he heard a voice saying,

*"Saul, Saul, why persecutest thou me?" (**Acts 9:4**)*

And he asked,

*Who art thou Lord? (**Acts 9:5**)*

Paul wanted to know the Person behind the voice. He must have thought, "Who is this person that wants to start leading me? I need to know him." He wanted to know the Person who had stopped him in his tracks and was now asking him to await further instructions. Suddenly, Paul had a new leader!

During that encounter, Jesus asked whether Paul could kick against the pricks—that is, kicking against nails—and not be injured? Paul got curious about everything that transpired at that moment and became desperate to learn more about 'this new Shepherd.' Though blind, Paul could perceive that this new Shepherd was different, awesome, and powerful!

Unlike Paul, many Christians today do not know the Lord!

> *"That the God of our Lord Jesus Christ, the Father of glory, may give unto you the spirit of wisdom and revelation in the knowledge of him:* [18]*The eyes of your understanding being enlightened; that ye may know what is the hope of his calling, and what the riches of the glory of his inheritance in the saints."* (***Ephesians 1:17-18***)

In these verses, Paul prayed for the Christians in Ephesus, and by extension, Christians worldwide and in every generation. He requested that God would give us the spirit of wisdom and revelation in the knowledge of Him, and that was his passion—to know the Lord! For him, nothing else could take precedence over this—the sheep must know their Shepherd.

John, the beloved, was arguably the closest Apostle to the Lord Jesus when He was here on the earth. As Jesus walked the face of the earth, multitudes followed Him. But there were the seventy, the twelve, the three, and then there was John, the beloved.

Closeness comes with relationship! The relationship between God's people and Christ is like marriage. You never know people until you live with them, stay under the same roof, and sleep and wake up together. Only then will you begin to see things that will make you say, "I did not know this or that about you."

Today, some people have almost left their marriage because they have found out some things about their spouse they never knew. Thus, it is good practice to wait on God for direction before entering into marriage. If God does not lead you into marriage or any other venture for that matter, you will be in trouble! God alone knows the end from the beginning! He knows your spouse-to-be, and indeed your spouse, more than you could ever find out because He created them.

Before marriage, a suitor comes to impress—he dresses well; everything is in order. Before you call, he would have arranged for lunch, for a drink, and all that sweetness. But after the wedding and a few short years later, you will be the one clamouring for an outing, and he will respond that he is tired from work and needs to rest. It will leave you wondering how things have changed! Beloved, God knows the right spouse for you!

On your own, making a choice might be influenced by *what you see*. But many of the people you may see or who may approach you may look good-natured and well-mannered in the public eye but are a different 'kettle of fish' when you interact with them privately, out of public glare! You cannot know any man or woman's real character from the outside—that is, by mere observation. Intimate knowledge comes with interaction!

*Knowing the Good Shepherd requires having information about Him, understanding, comprehending, and applying that information to our everyday living.*

Now, back to John. John thought he knew Christ because He would speak in parables when He talked to the multitude, and the people would not understand. Jesus had some seventy disciples to whom He would decode some of the parables. However, Jesus reserved more profound revelation and more open explanation in plain language for the twelve. Then one day, He told all of them: "Look, from henceforth, I no longer call you servants, but friends, because you know details about me; you know secrets about me." (**John 15:15**).

Not all of the twelve saw Jesus at the mount of transfiguration. He took only Peter, James and John, and they got more revelation of Him as a result. He took these three to the mountain to pray, but they were sleepy. When they awoke, right before their eyes, they saw Jesus transfigured into a divine Being! No one else saw that, except Peter, James, and John! They not only saw Jesus transfigured, but they heard a voice from heaven saying,

*"This is my beloved Son, hear him!" (**Mark 9:7**)*

Thus, these three knew Jesus deeper than the others! Yet in later years, on the island of Patmos, John was to have an encounter with Jesus and did not recognize Him! On the Isle of Patmos, a place where John was exiled, Jesus appeared to him, and it was a frightful sight; John did not recognize the Lord. He saw Jesus, but it was not the same Jesus he had known while He was on the earth.

If John were that intimate with Christ, should he not have recognized Him the first time on the Isle of Patmos? There are levels or depths of revelation involved in knowing the Lord.

On the Isle of Patmos, John saw Jesus Christ, Who told him, "What you see, write; I am going to show you what is happening now, and what will happen later." As you read the Book of Revelation, you can see the depth of what the Lord Jesus opened up to John.

John's description of his encounter with the Lord was of a different dimension! Hear him:

> "His head and his hairs were white like wool, as white as snow; and his eyes were as a flame of fire; ¹⁵And his feet like unto fine brass, as if they burned in a furnace; and his voice as the sound of many waters. ¹⁶And he had in his right hand seven stars: and out of his mouth went a sharp two-edged sword: and his countenance was as the sun shineth in his strength. ¹⁷And when I saw him, I fell at his feet as dead. And he laid his right hand upon me, saying unto me, "Fear not; I am the first and the last: ¹⁸I am he that liveth, and was dead; and behold, I am alive for evermore, Amen; and have the keys of hell and of death. ¹⁹Write the things which thou hast seen, and the things which are, and the things which shall be hereafter" (**Revelation 1:14-19**)

John did not know before then that the Lord is the Ancient of Days, the oldest *man* that ever lived! He wrote that the Lord's eyes were like a flame of fire because He dwells in the fire! His voice was like the sound of many waters, His feet were like fine brass, and His countenance was like the sun shining in its highest intensity! Of course, He is the Sun of Righteousness! The point is, John found out new things about Christ.

In the same way, you need to know Him more. I do not know what you already know of Him, but you can still know more like Paul and John! Your knowledge of Christ is so crucial. You must know Him! The closer you are to Christ, the more of Him you will know!

*Closeness comes with relationship! Intimate knowledge comes with interaction!*

Mary and Martha thought they knew Jesus because He was close to them. He went to their home and was a family friend. Yet, they did not know Him because, as we saw earlier when Jesus arrived after Lazarus was dead, Mary believed that if Jesus had been there, her brother would not have died, while Martha believed that Lazarus would rise again on the Last Day. But they did not know Him enough to realise that He is the Resurrection and the Life and that His presence in their midst was good news! They did not know about the part where Jesus can reverse the irreversible!

Jesus told Martha that only one thing was critical: to pay attention to His words rather than being engrossed in serving. He told Martha that Mary had chosen the right path by sitting at His feet to listen to His teaching and that she had received something vital, which she could not lose (**Luke 10:38-42**). The right path which Mary chose is *the knowledge path*.

But when Jesus raised Lazarus from the dead after four days, He not only proved to be the Resurrection and the Life (**John 11:1-45**) but for Mary and Martha, that was a whole new level of *knowing* the Good Shepherd.

There is a new revelation for someone reading this book because the Lord has assured me that everything dead in your life will come back to life—specifically, a brother whose genitalia had died; God says to tell you that it is back to normal!

If you are the one who has been going to the hospital and they told you your kidney, heart, and vital organs are dead, as you read this, I want you to have faith because I declare them restored in Jesus name. Your liver and vital organs will begin to function well again in the mighty name of Jesus. He is reversing the irreversible in your life now for good!

That cancer growth is dead now in the name of Jesus. Jesus is restoring your joy because He is the Resurrection and the Life.

You who think that your marriage is over, I decree in the name of Jesus who died and rose again that there will be a turnaround. That dead womb has come alive in the name of Jesus!

Sarah did not know Him. When God told her that she would be pregnant at the age of ninety, she laughed. She did not know about the Resurrection and the Life. Menopause is said to be the cessation of productivity for every woman experiencing it. That is according to the language of doctors. But they have never written it as *'menostop'* because they do not know. If they say it is a *pause*, that means that it is indeed not a cessation, but a break and regular services can resume—your age is irrelevant when God is involved!

Regardless of what you have been told or heard, as you read this, I can assure you that the resurrection power is present there with you, to manifest if only you can believe and accept this knowledge. I declare that all dead organs in your system should live again from this moment in the name of Jesus.

*The closer you are to Christ, the more of Him you will know!*

David, as a shepherd boy, spent much time with the Lord. He wrote several Psalms about his intimate relationship with the Lord. He also spent much time meditating on the word of God, yet in **2 Samuel 6:2-11**, David decided to transport the Ark of the LORD using a new cart—a violation of God's instruction on how the Ark of the LORD's presence was to moved! To make matters worse, as the procession was singing and praising God, the cart upon which they placed the Ark stumbled, and the Ark shook. Uzzah then put forth his hand to steady the Ark, and God struck him dead right there! It was a fearful thing, even for King David and the people of Israel!

When you know God, you will realise that He is holy and fearful—this is very instructive! If you are sinning, do not even bother to praise God because if you do, He can kill you! He is fearful in praises. He inhabits the praises of His people, but He is also of purer eyes than to behold iniquity (**Habakkuk 1:13**). So, you cannot invite Him while singing praises only for Him to come and find you dirty!

## MANY OF GOD'S PEOPLE DO NOT UNDERSTAND HIM!

In **2 Samuel 6:1-15**, David misfired by daring to carry the Ark of God with a cart! God had given instruction on how the Ark was to be transported, so how did David get his methodology? The procedure God instituted involved the priests carrying the Ark, using staves slid into its sides, on their shoulders. None was to touch or move the Ark besides the priests! And here, David, the king, who supposedly knew God, was violating His instructions! The point is we can get too familiar with God and end up thinking that we can do anything and that He will accept it! No! He will not!

The Bible records that God was incensed against them, and He smote

Uzzah, who dared to touch the Ark!

> *"And David and all the house of Israel played before the*
> *LORD on all manner of instruments made of fir wood,*
> *even on harps, and on psalteries, and on timbrels, and on*
> *cornets, and on cymbals. ⁶And when they came to Nachon's*
> *threshing floor, Uzzah put forth his hand to the ark of God,*
> *and took hold of it; for the oxen shook it. ⁷And the anger*
> *of the LORD was kindled against Uzzah; and God smote*
> *him there for his error; and there he died by the ark of God.*
> *⁸And David was displeased, because the LORD had made*
> *a breach upon Uzzah: and he called the name of the place*
> *Perezuzzah to this day. ⁹And David was afraid of the LORD*
> *that day, and said, How shall the ark of the LORD come to*
> *me?" (2 Samuel 6:5-9)*

When God struck, David moved back. He was afraid of God! He did not know that you cannot fool around with sin or act presumptuously and hang around God—this applies to anyone who is a Christian! Do not hang around God if you are fooling around with sin. Our God is a consuming *God's presence is 'the' blessing!* fire! He can consume you in a flash. That much, David discovered in a moment.

After Uzzah died, they took the Ark to the house of one Obededom. I suspect that Obededom, as the Ark was on its way to his house, must have got up to instruct and 'sanctify' everybody in his household. He must have told his people, "Look, God is coming to live here, and when He comes, you cannot afford to live anyhow! You must have heard that He just killed Uzzah, and because David must hate me, he is bringing Him here!" That certainly would have caused a significant transformation in that house because if the children were stubborn, they had to change. Likewise, if his wife was a trouble-maker, she had to make adjustments. Everybody had to start behaving well. They knew that if they did not conduct themselves aright, they would die! In other words, there would be praise and worship every morning. There would be constant fellowship. If Obededom called his wife, she would have to answer sweetly, saying, "Yes, honey!" Everybody will be well-behaved! All this would be because God was in the house! And the scriptures say that "God blessed Obededom and his household!"

---

Many people fail to understand that when they live right, God will establish them. Many children of God are carrying Him inside them, but they always forget what that truly means. A husband who has God on the inside and shouting, "Stupid woman!" at his wife forgets that God heard that! That is why David wrote with understanding when he said,

*"I have set the LORD always before me: because he is at my right hand, I shall not be moved." (**Psalm 16:8**)*

*You cannot be living in sin and still call yourself a child of God!*

If you know that, then you will understand that there are many things that you cannot say. That is because God knows, sees, and hears everything, including your thoughts! Hence, it is folly to think that you can shut your door and do things, and God will not see you! No way! If this is how you reason, then it shows that you do not know God. If you did, you would not take such dangerous chances.

The preceding creates a valid point about why the sheep must *know* the Shepherd. You must be aware of Whose you are in a relationship. Obededom ensured that his household lived right while the ark was in his house, and indeed, afterwards. He was sanctifying them and getting them prepared for God. As a result of their preparation, God had barely entered into their lives before they began enjoying new levels of divine blessings! Unfortunately, several Christians today are standing in the way of God's blessings for them without realising that God's presence is 'the' blessing!

Every child of God is a carrier of His presence, but many are dealing with it casually. They treat His presence with levity because they do not know Him. Our God is a consuming fire! Sure, He is a God of love and mercy, but do not ever take Him for granted—you cannot afford to risk that. It is ignorant people that would dare take Him for granted.

There was this story in the news some time ago about two people who went into an old church building to have sex. They did not think to go to a brothel or motel; it was inside the building where God meets with His people they chose. While engaging in their abominable act, a pillar in the building gave way, fell on them, killing them instantly! And the question someone was asking was, "why would someone go into a church building to fornicate?" It is because they do not know God! They had no regard for God, nor did they fear Him! Someone who calls himself a child of God would not do that. First of all, they would not want to sin because they have the Spirit of God dwelling in them. Even if they made mistakes, they would immediately get the signal to ask God for forgiveness.

You cannot be living in sin and still call yourself a child of God! A carrier of His presence? Only if you don't know God will you be toying with sin and desire His company. If you know God, you will not live a life of sin and iniquity.

Jonah knew God to be merciful, so when God told him to go and preach to the people of Nineveh, he replied, "If I go and tell these people about your plan to destroy them, they will repent, and you will change your mind!" He knew God is very merciful, but he did not realise that there was nowhere on planet earth that anyone could hide from God. Instead of going to Nineveh, Jonah headed for Tarshish on a ship, running away from God—what a futile mission! God intercepted the ship; the storm, wind, and waves all responded to God's command. Eventually, God prepared a fish to swallow Jonah after he was thrown overboard and was there for three days—in the belly of the fish!

Jonah was to find out later that apart from being merciful, God is in total control of all things, and there is no running away from Him. He also knew that he could not hide from God!

There is the story of a brother who had been born-again for several years but got fed up and thought to himself: "Look, this *born-again* thing is not working; that is how one day I would go to heaven and miss all the fun on planet earth; all in the name of being born again. I've been born again for ten years now; let me enjoy myself a little." So, he went to the U.K. When he got there, he did not tell anyone that he was a Christian. He started living wildly, going to night clubs and living the life of a party pooper. One night, as he entered a night club, he saw Jesus, and the Lord told him point-blank, "*I am waiting for you!*"

You cannot run from the Lord—He loves you enough to "wait" for you and save you!

The sheep must *know* the Shepherd. Moses prayed, "God, let me know you." Whenever I remember this prayer, I say to myself, "See Moses, of all people, praying this kind of prayer, what else does he want to know about God? He had gone to God and spent forty days and nights with Him on two distinct occasions. He had been on the mountain of God, and the Bible says that God spoke to him face to face, as a man speaks to his friend." Still, Moses prayed, "God, if I have found grace in your sight, show me Your glory!" (**Exodus 33:17-18**). Imagine Moses' hunger and passion for the knowledge of God!

Do you have a burning desire to know God like Moses? He was desperate to know his God, and that was why, after all the encounters he had had with God, he could still pray, "Let me know you!" God, in His love and mercy, told Moses, "Okay, I will do you a favour. I will teach you my ways." And the Bible says God taught Moses His ways, but the children of Israel only saw His acts (**Psalm 103:7**).

There is a difference between God's ways and God's deeds. God's ways relate to His Personality, Nature, or Character, while His acts refer to His doings. We learn about God's deeds by seeing what He does—His miracles, signs, and wonders.

Moses got confused at a point, wondering why God would invest so much in bringing the Israelites out of Egypt and then decide to kill them all because of sin. He found out that God's nature abhors sin! God loves you but hates your sin. He is a Holy God who keeps and honours His word. When God says He will do a thing, He does it! He is not a man who promises and fails. God is a Holy God!

The Psalmist writes:

> *"I will worship toward thy holy temple, and praise thy name for thy loving kindness and for thy truth: for thou hast magnified thy word above all thy name."* (***Psalm 138:2***)

So, as God has spoken,

> *"the soul that sinneth, it shall die."* (***Ezekiel 18:4***)

The children of Israel had sinned, and God had seen it, so He was set to judge them! But Moses said, "O Lord, will You destroy your people despite all the things that you have done for them in the past? Now, will people say, it is because you cannot get them to the promised land, that is why you left them in the wilderness to die!"

There were things Moses did not know about God; therefore, he prayed, "If I have found grace in your sight, show me now thy way, let me know You." So, He taught Moses His ways.

You need to know God. Many of God's people today do not read the Bible. They do not invest time to know God. You need to read the Bible to get information about God. If you have never read it before, start today! If you read it like a 'storybook', get 'the story', understand 'the story', and then study it to intimate yourself about the 'story'.

> *"Study to shew thyself approved unto God, a workman that needeth not to be ashamed, rightly dividing the word of truth." (**2 Timothy 2:15**)*

It says, *"to show thyself approved unto God."* Knowing the Shepherd as your Creator is of paramount importance. Hence, to show yourself approved unto God does not stop at merely reading the Bible; you need to take it to another dimension, which is to meditate:

> *"This book of the law shall not depart out of thy mouth; but thou shalt meditate therein day and night, that thou mayest observe to do according to all that is written therein: for then thou shalt make thy way prosperous, and then thou shalt have good success." (**Joshua 1:8**)*

Again, you need to emulate the man in **Psalm 1:1-2**:

> *"Blessed is the man that walketh not in the counsel of the ungodly, nor standeth in the way of sinners, nor sitteth in the seat of the scornful. ²But his delight is in the law of the LORD; and in his law doth he meditate day and night."*

Like sheep, you must acquire knowledge about God, gain a deeper understanding of who He is and maintain a vibrant relationship with Him.

# THE FOUNDATION OF KNOWING GOD

Two people cannot walk together, except they agree (**Amos 3:3**). To have a relationship with God, therefore, you must be born again. That is the starting point for beginning the journey of knowing God. There is no other entry point.

In comparing marriage to our relationship with God, Paul stressed the maxim of leaving to cleave; that is, only after you 'leave' can you cleave, or as the scripture says,

> *Therefore shall a man leave his father and mother and shall cleave unto his wife. (**Genesis** 2:24)*

You will have to leave the world before you can cleave unto Jesus! And when you cleave unto Him, you will know Him. You cannot be one leg outside—in the world—and one leg inside—in Christ. When you get this revelation, you will know that you need to cleave unto Him wholly. When you cleave to Jesus, applied knowledge comes to play because you can read the Bible with a deeper understanding of who God is, and this will instruct and guide your affairs in life. You will be able to sit down and hear the word, and the word will transform your life immediately and forever.

I pray that God will open Himself unto you and give you the spirit of wisdom and revelation in the knowledge of Him.

> *"The eyes of your understanding being enlightened; that ye may know what is the hope of his calling, and what the riches of the glory of his inheritance in the saints." (**Ephesians** 1:18)*

Paul prayed that we might enter into a depth of revelation in the knowledge of Christ! Oh, the benefits of this level of knowing Christ! When you attain this knowledge of Christ, you will not mistakenly follow another. With this level of knowing God, you can walk into a group meeting and know whether or not God is present at the meeting. It will not even matter who the pastor is or what he is saying.

Nowadays, people go to strange places to receive fake power to perform magic and build a 'church' to make money. But as someone who God leads, you can walk into such a place and instantly know that the Spirit of God is not there. You cannot be deceived!

When you know Him, you will become His friend, just like Abraham and Moses. Of Abraham, God said:

> *"And the LORD said, "Shall I hide from Abraham that thing which I do; [18]Seeing that Abraham shall surely become a great and mighty nation, and all the nations of the earth shall be blessed in him? [19]For I know him, that he will command his children and his household after him, and they shall keep the way of the LORD, to do justice and judgment; that the LORD may bring upon Abraham that which he hath spoken of him." (**Genesis 18:17-19**)*

How can God call someone, His friend? When some people pray about their forefathers, they usually ask God to forgive their sins of idolatry and so on. When I am gone, my children can pray, "Father, remember Bayo, your friend forever...!" — this is my prayer; my heart's desire! There should be no need to pray for forgiveness of the sins of the forefathers.

*You will have to leave the world before you can cleave unto Jesus!*

That is how Jehoshaphat prayed:

> *"And said, O LORD God of our fathers, art not thou God in heaven? And rulest not thou over all the kingdoms of the heathen? and in thine hand is there not power and might, so that none is able to withstand thee? [7]Art not thou our God, who didst drive out the inhabitants of this land before thy people Israel, and gavest it to the seed of Abraham thy friend for ever?" (**2 Chronicles 20:6-7**)*

I recall how my grandfather, who was born again, would come to our house at 4 a.m. and would knock on the door continuously until we opened. Then, he would have a thirty-minute fellowship with us, leave a word and then move on. When he was getting ready to depart this world, someone went to his bedside and said, "Baba, you are dying," he replied, "I can never die!" He had the revelation that saints do not die; they only fall asleep!

Close to his departure from this world, my grandfather gave me his Bible, but I did not understand the import then. I just dropped the Bible somewhere. But today, this calling that I thought was an accident, I now know was a passing of the baton to me! That was the significance of my grandfather's action—he did not give it to his son, my father, who only became saved a few months before his decease; he gave it to me!

# THE BENEFITS OF KNOWING GOD

He revealed to Abraham His plan to destroy Sodom and Gomorrah. He got into a very intimate discussion with him, which allowed Abraham to intercede to salvage the situation. There are secrets that God reveals to those who are close to Him.

*Nothing will faze you when you know the Good Shepherd!*

The Sunday before the Late General Sani Abacha died, my Area Pastor at the time went for evangelism in one of the Lekki villages, which is now very well developed. When they got to the village, an old woman came to the pastor and said, "That man Abacha, God is taking him out tomorrow!" And it happened as she had said! God had revealed it to her as she had been praying before then.

Also, when you are close to God, you will be at peace. Nothing will faze you when you know Him because you will know what He will do—He will reveal it to you.

# HOW CAN I KNOW GOD?

The starting point to acquiring the knowledge of God is through being born again. So, how do you become born again? You are born again when the Spirit of God gives birth to a new human spirit in you. Your dead spirit comes alive, and you can relate with God, spirit to Spirit.

> *"For what man knoweth the things of a man, save the spirit of man which is in him? Even so the things of God knoweth no man, but the Spirit of God"* (**1 Corinthians 2:11**)

If someone who does not know anything about me asks to know my name, if my response is "Segun" instead of "Bayo", only my spirit knows that I am lying. In the same vein, no one knows the things of God except God's Spirit. It is the Spirit of God that knows God! And because you are a regenerated spirit, you have access to God's Spirit, and you can know God. Therefore, you get to know God through your spirit when you become born again because you now have access to God's Spirit.

There is a depth that you can tap into in God, but it must first begin with being born again. Through being born again, you enter into a relationship with God through Jesus Christ. You need this relationship with God above all else, and then you must grow in this relationship with Him. The Bible says:

> *"This I say then, "Walk in the Spirit, and ye shall not fulfil the lust of the flesh." (**Galatians 5:16**)*

Walking in the Spirit is the Holy Spirit giving you direction on what to do and where to go. By having access to God's Spirit, you become close to Him, and He, to you. You are also enabled to please Him and live sin-free. And as a result, your requests will be readily granted. And as you grow in your relationship and desire to know Him more, He will reveal more of Himself to you, and your knowledge of Him will continue to grow!

# Chapter 8

**The Good Shepherd**

# The Hearing Dimension

*I know His voice,*

*my Saviour's voice;*
*And oh, it makes*

*my heart rejoice,*
*Whenever He*

*shall speak to me;*
*O praise the Lord*

*I know His voice.*


*Refrain for "Though I my Savior may not see"*
*(1902)*

*by Johnson Oatman Jr., 1856–1922*

Our goal in this book is to teach how to live a successful and productive life. In a book titled *"How You Can Be Led By The Spirit of God,"* by Kenneth E. Hagin, which I recommend to you, Kenneth E. Hagin writes about one time when Jesus appeared to him in his house. Before then, he was struggling with a thought in his heart: a local assembly had invited him to minister, and each time he would try to respond to them that he would come, he would stop midway and tear up the paper. He tore it three times before he decided that he was not going to that church to minister.

Sharing about the encounter, Hagin wrote that when Jesus entered his house, He sat down and said to him:

> "You see Me sitting here talking to you…you are seeing into the realm of the spirit. You see Me. You hear Me talking. I am bringing you, through the vision, a word of knowledge and also a word of wisdom. I am telling you not to go to that church. The pastor would not accept the way you will minister when you get there. But I am never going to lead you this way again … From now on, I am going to lead you by the inward witness. You had the inward witness all the time. You had a check in your spirit. That is the reason you tore up the letter three times. You had something on the inside, a check, a red light, a stop signal. It was not even a voice that said, 'Do not go.' It was just an inward intuition."[1]

Hagin narrated that Jesus further told him He would make him rich by His Spirit, but he must follow every instruction of the Holy Spirit.

This introduction is to show you what being led by God's Spirit is all about. Essentially, it is about how to be successful in life God's way. It is about how to reach your goal and fulfil divine destiny.

Jesus told Hagin clearly what to do. To bolster the import of getting God's approval before taking decisions of any magnitude, Hagin, in his book, cited examples of people he knew who would not make a single investment without first confirming that it was what God wanted them to do! I recommend that you read the book to understand the subject of

1    Kenneth E. Hagin, How You Can Be Led By The Spirit of God, p.30-31

being led by God's Spirit.

I am laying the foundation for our discussion in this chapter. We shall be discussing how the Good Shepherd can lead us through the Holy Spirit.

# FOLLOWING THE LEADING OF THE HOLY SPIRIT

It is fundamental to understand that the Good Shepherd is good and leads aright always. He knows the end from the beginning as He is the Alpha and Omega. Human beings are limited in knowledge; hence, their need to *follow* One who knows it all—the Good Shepherd by His Spirit. When you follow the Holy Spirit, you can never go wrong. If you knew the answers to all the questions in life, life would be a lot easier for you. And this is what the Good Shepherd through the Holy Spirit brings to the table.

In Nigeria several years ago, many people were oblivious that there could be another way of packaging drinking water for sale, other than in plastic bottles and large dispensing cans. However, someone arose one day and started selling water in nylon sachets, now popularly known as "pure water." As it stands today, "pure water" is the most consumed packaged water in Nigeria! With an estimated turnover of over Seven billion Naira daily.[2] Can you imagine what has become of those who started that business today? I am sure that they are made for life—speaking financially!

*The Spirit of God Who lives within the believer leads him.*

That is why I am telling you how important it is for you to just listen to the Spirit of God because it will usher you into a new dimension of reality. Whilst I make no pretensions that the pioneers of the "pure water" industry are Christians, I can aver that such is the kind of idea that can come from the Holy Spirit to one of His own. The difficulty is that when the Holy Spirit reveals such basic concepts to some Christians, they usually disdain them, leaving God no other alternative than to hand it over to those who are open to receive it, even if they are not Christians (**John 1:11-12**)!

---

2    https://technext.ng/2019/08/02/streettech-pure-water-production-and-nafdac-how-safe-do-you-think-your-water-is/

In my personal experience in the last several years, I do not take any significant step without God. I have taken some steps that were supposedly strange steps that made someone say, "This guy is mad!"

I will give you an example: This happened while working for an oil firm where I was the Eastern Region Manager. Apart from my car, a Peugeot 504, I had a driver and a personal military escort, besides the several posted to the station. In addition to that, there were five other cars which I had access to any time I wanted. Then something happened! The Holy Spirit said I should leave the place. So, I followed His leading and went to work for another oil company in Warri.

Upon arriving at this new job, there was a six-month probation period before any benefits could accrue my way. Imagine a guy like me that had all those perks at my former job. So, what did I do? I would go to Warri by public bus. I would not take the 504. The way they packed people in buses at Warri then was quite discomforting. On a row of seats meant for only three passengers, they would load four persons. The front seat, which should have taken one passenger, took two passengers, packing commuters like *sardines*! That was my new life after I had lived in relative comfort at my previous job.

That was how I transported myself to and from the new job within the six-month probation period in Warri. I would come to Owerri from Warri, and when I arrived, I would take a bike to my house. Some of the people who saw me—people who were working for me while I was at the firm with the juicy perks—would say, "This man has gone mad!" They were asking themselves, "How can someone leave that kind of job?" But God told me to go to Warri for a purpose.

It turned out that six months after working in Warri, one of my former bosses at the last job had moved on to work for another indigenous company. Before he left, he was expressly told: "You cannot hire anybody from this company to work for you." He signed the document that contained that clause. And then he had the challenge of needing quality people to work for him in the new company but could not poach any staff from the former firm because of that 'non-compete clause' that he had signed. But because I had left that company before him and had moved to Warri, I became the only person he could engage in his new assignment. God's *plan* was becoming more evident.

That was how my former boss came and invited me to work for him. I told him about other people who were more proficient than me when it came to performing the work, but he said he could not ask any of them because he had signed a 'non-compete clause!' He told me that I was the only one who had left my former company and was not bound by the clause. That was what made him come to me. To God's glory, he gave me a big job as Operations Manager and moved me from Warri to Port Harcourt. When I got to Port Harcourt, they moved me straight to the Presidential Hotel, where I lodged for several months at the Company's expense! A car was given to me and upgraded to a jeep after six months. It was just from one level of upgrade to another.

*If you are born again and sanctified, you are spiritual. You do not have to be looking for 'spectacular' signs every day.*

For context, maybe a little picture of the organogram in a typical oil firm would help you understand the movement from my former company's level before I went to Warri and what the new offer in Port Harcourt brought. At the top, you have the Managing Director, then the Deputy Managing Director, Operations Manager, Production Manager, and so on, down the chart. I was just the Manager in charge of one of the fields in my former company. But after what was a step down to Warri, I was now catapulted to the position of Operations Manager. And much more than the new office's perks, the view from the top was completely different!

I am sharing this testimony because when *God led me into making the transition*, I did not understand it. It seemed to me like; how could you go from bad to worse? But then, God said it was alright. There was a purpose for it. That is why, when God is leading you, you can never go wrong! People can look at you and say, "What is this man doing?" You just put your trust in God completely.

God told Elijah that a widow would feed him, but when he got to the widow's house, she was gathering sticks for her last meal! Isn't that a laugh? Can God be wrong? Certainly not! But Elijah got there and met stark hunger, and that was where God had sent him!

Likewise, some people would find themselves in a company with no form or comeliness, and they will say, "How can God bring me to this place?" The truth is that if that company were so great, the entry conditions would be too stringent, and you probably would not get a position there. That is why God has brought you in at that point so that when things begin to improve, you will have the opportunity to grow with the organization, garner experience, and have value in your field of endeavour!

God works in ways you cannot understand; all that is required is to follow the Spirit of God. That is all you need to do. Do not question the Good Shepherd; just follow Him.

# THE KEY TO FOLLOWING THE HOLY SPIRIT'S LEADING

*"Verily, verily, I say unto you, He that entereth not by the door into the sheepfold, but climbeth up some other way, the same is a thief and a robber. ²But he that entereth in by the door is the shepherd of the sheep. ³To him the porter openeth; and the sheep hear his voice: and he calleth his own sheep by name, and leadeth them out. ⁴And when he putteth forth his own sheep, he goeth before them, and the sheep follow him: for they know his voice. ⁵And a stranger will they not follow, but will flee from him: for they know not the voice of strangers. ⁶This parable spake Jesus unto them: but they understood not what things they were which he spake unto them." (John 10:1-6)*

In *v. 4*, when speaking about the sheep and the shepherd, Jesus said, "… *they know his voice.*" The key to *following* is to know the voice of the Good Shepherd as distinct from other voices. Because the Good Shepherd is a Spirit, He leads the sheep through the spirit. If you want to be led by the Good Shepherd, therefore, you must be spiritual. The Good Shepherd's voice is the Spirit of God's voice because God is a Spirit (**John 4:24**).

By divine design, the sheep is spirit, soul, and body. The sheep can hear the 'voice' of the body, which is 'the feeling', the 'voice' of the soul, which is 'reasoning' and the 'voice' of the human spirit, which is 'conscience'. The sheep can hear all three. The question then is: "How can the sheep continue to hear the voice of the Holy Spirit amidst those other voices?" The sheep must operate in the spirit! There is zero room for carnality or sensuality. The sheep must be spiritually sensitive to be able to hear the voice of the Good Shepherd.

Of course, many people would prefer that God speak to them in a 'spectacular' way. That way, they think that they will not make a mistake. So, if God were to call out your name, and you turned around and saw nobody, you would be sure that it is God? "Wow," you may say with excitement, "He just called me!". Therefore, anything God says, you would do it straight away because it was easy to hear from Him. You will not need to read the Bible; all you will have to do, is wait till He calls out your name again? But then, God calls unbelievers too. So then, what would differentiate your own experience from an unbeliever's, if God had to bellow your name each time He wanted to communicate with you?

The Spirit of God Who lives within the believer leads him. He does not require any dramatization of communication with God.

Being led by the Holy Spirit is a special privilege for believers because when He leads an unbeliever, He would appear in a vision or a dream. For Saul of Tarsus, also known as Paul, when God took hold of him, He intercepted him in an open vision encounter. Today, many Christians are looking for signs, which is not fitting for them; this is what you expect of unbelievers. As a parent, if you have three children—the first one being a very stubborn child; the second, quite miserly; and, the third one, being a very great child: when visitors come to your home, and you want to address the stubborn one, most parents will likely shout and say, "go and do this or that!" On the contrary, you will use a sign or body language to pass your message to the very great and quiet child. You will not need to scream and shout to get him or her to do your bidding! In the same vein, the 'Sauls' of this world need noise. But like the quiet child, you are not one of the 'Sauls' of this world; you are spiritual already.

If you are born again and sanctified, you are spiritual. You do not have to be looking for 'spectacular' signs every day. The danger of looking for signs is that you will become dependent on them, and any time you do not see the signs, you will not believe that it is God leading you. I pray that God will change that mindset in your life in Jesus name.

So, the key to following the Holy Spirit's leading is to be spiritual, which happens when you are born again and sanctified—this is the starting point. Next, you need to be able to decipher the voice of God.

# UNDERSTANDING GOD'S VOICE

How does the voice of God sound? In the Book of Revelation, John says that His voice is like

*"the sound of many waters!" (**Revelation 1:15**)*

So, if He is going to speak to you, perhaps you would expect Him to roar like the ocean? In other words, if it is not booming, then it is not God? Is it not John trying to describe the sound that he heard when God was speaking? Are you peradventure waiting for that kind of experience when God speaks to you? That is the kind of dramatic encounter most of us desire, but the reality is quite different.

Knowing the voice of God begins with the spiritual birth—you must be born again! I cannot stress this enough. Because you are a tripartite being—spirit, soul, and body—you hear God most effectively when you are in the Spirit. In the garden of Eden, God told Adam that if he ate of the fruit of the tree of the knowledge of good and evil, he would die. They disobeyed and *died*, albeit spiritually, after eating the fruit that God had asked not to eat. But they were still conscious in the soulish realm and even had their body. The Bible records that they both realised that they were naked and covered their bodies with leaves. What died in them was their *spirit*. Hence, they told God that they were hiding from Him—because they were naked, and their bodies were still alive. This realization proves that their mental or soul realm was working though their spirit was *dead*.

*The salvation experience is the Spirit of God awakening our dead spirit; the sanctification experience is the Spirit of God removing our old Adamic nature that loves to sin and replacing it with the divine nature that loves and obeys God.*

So, Adam and Eve died a spiritual death in the garden of Eden, and this is where Jesus came in to restore us to God:

*"... Except a man be born again, he cannot see the kingdom of God. ... Except a man be born of water and of the Spirit,*

*he cannot enter into the kingdom of God. That which is*
*born of the flesh is flesh; and that which is born of the Spirit*
*is spirit. (John 3:3-6)*

You have to be born again for your spirit to be alive. In other words, if a man has to walk with God, then he must be born again. The spiritual walk begins with salvation. The initial Christian experience has two dimensions: The first dimension is being born of the Spirit—which is when the Spirit of God gives birth to a new human spirit in you. Your spirit experiences a rebirth, meaning that the Spirit of God has regenerated your human spirit. That is the first experience when you come in contact with the Holy Spirit. The second experience is when the Holy Spirit indwells you. From then on, the Holy Spirit will commence sanctifying and transforming you into the image and likeness of Christ.

Let us consider these experiences in some detail.

## THE SALVATION EXPERIENCE

*… as many as received him, to them gave he power to be-*
*come the sons of God, even to them that believe on his name:*
*Which were born, not of blood, nor of the will of the flesh,*
*nor of the will of man, but of God. (John 1:12-13)*

*Whosoever is born of God doth not commit sin; for his seed*
*remaineth in him: and he cannot sin, because he is born of*
*God. (1 John 3:9)*

These verses of scripture speak of the new birth as being born of the Spirit of God. That is, the DNA of God is now in you. This action re-awakens the spirit of man that died in the Garden of Eden. One of the immediate signs you will experience is peace and joy and a hatred for the things you did when you were not born again.

## THE SANCTIFICATION EXPERIENCE

*"Jesus answered and said unto her, "If thou knewest the gift*
*of God, and who it is that saith to thee, Give me to drink;*
*thou wouldest have asked of him, and he would have giv-*
*en thee living water." ¹¹The woman saith unto him, "Sir,*
*thou hast nothing to draw with, and the well is deep: from*
*whence then hast thou that living water? ¹²Art thou greater*

*than our father Jacob, which gave us the well, and drank thereof himself, and his children, and his cattle?" [13]Jesus answered and said unto her, "Whosoever drinketh of this water shall thirst again: [14]But whosoever drinketh of the water that I shall give him shall never thirst; but the water that I shall give him shall be in him a well of water springing up into everlasting life." (**John 4:10-14**)*

*"In the last day, that great day of the feast, Jesus stood and cried, saying, "If any man thirst, let him come unto me, and drink. [38]He that believeth on me, as the scripture hath said, out of his belly shall flow rivers of living water." [39](But this spake he of the Spirit, which they that believe on him should receive: for the Holy Ghost was not yet given; because that Jesus was not yet glorified." (**John 7:37-39**)*

These verses of scripture speak about *"the in-filling or sanctification experience."* The salvation experience is the Spirit of God within us, awakening our dead spirit. In contrast, the sanctification experience is the Spirit of God within us, removing our old Adamic nature that loves to sin and replacing it with the divine nature that loves and obeys God.

Such is the action of *"the well of water springing forth"* and *"living water out of the belly"*. Once you have gone through the second experience, the Holy Ghost is very much in you! Your spirit is reborn of God, and you have unimpeded access to God!

Recall that I shared earlier that you can never lie to your spirit. Every time you tell a lie, something knows the truth; and that is your spirit! Now, because you have a reborn spirit that the Spirit of God is sanctifying, you have access to God through that reborn spirit. It knows the mind of God through the Spirit of God. At this point, you can connect with God—your spirit talking to God's Spirit!

Once you are born again, the Spirit of God comes to indwell you. But He is indwelling you to remove vestiges of the old life which remains, even though you are born again. Removing the remnants of the old life is sanctification, and it makes us able to obey God. It also makes it possible to hear God or, better still, be in constant communication with God. From thenceforth, you are ready to be led by the Holy Spirit!

# HOW THE GOOD SHEPHERD LEADS THE SHEEP BY HIS SPIRIT

When Jesus was about to go to the cross, He told His disciples that He would be with them, even after He would have departed. And when one of them asked Him how that would happen, He told them that it would essentially be by His Spirit. So, when we are born again, and the Holy Spirit comes to take up residence within us, it is Jesus, the Good Shepherd, in us by His Spirit—which is the Holy Spirit, who is also known as the Spirit of God (**1 Corinthians 2:10-11**) or the Spirit of Christ (**Romans 8:9**).

So, as we look at being led by the Good Shepherd, we are practically speaking of a spiritual leading by His Spirit—the Holy Spirit. We have outlined seven ways by which the Holy Spirit can lead us.

## 1. THE INWARD WITNESS

> *"For as many as are led by the Spirit of God, they are the sons of God. ¹⁵For ye have not received the spirit of bondage again to fear; but ye have received the Spirit of adoption, whereby we cry, Abba, Father. ¹⁶The Spirit itself beareth witness with our spirit, that we are the children of God:"* (*Romans 8:14-16*)

As many as are responding to the Holy Spirit's leading; these are the sons of God! There is communication between you and the Good Shepherd because the Spirit bears witness with your spirit that this is taking place. It is like an internet connection indicator on our mobile phones that indicates a link between the mobile phone and the world wide web.

So, one of the ways God leads us is through the *'spiritual man'*—that is, the spirit man who lives inside your physical body. He leads you by the *'inward witness.'* He is the One on your inside acting as a check—restraining or releasing you (giving you the "go-ahead") —on any issue concerning your life. It is either a red light—restraint—or a green light—release. It comes from within. You do not feel it; you just know it is on your inside.

> *"Now when much time was spent, and when sailing was*

> now dangerous, because the fast was now already past, Paul admonished them, [10]And said unto them, Sirs, I perceive that this voyage will be with hurt and much damage, not only of the lading and ship, but also of our lives." (**Acts 27:9-10**)

The phrase in this scripture is, *"I perceive."* Please pay close attention to this phrase to understand where we are going and appreciate what we are communicating here. Let us bring Paul's mission forward to our present Age and say that you want to make a move. Let us say you are going to Abuja and need to catch a flight, and there is a red light from the inward witness, and you *"perceive"* that you should not make the trip. Whatever happens, when you go ahead with the trip, the reaction of many people would not be far from, "Oh! And he had said that he did not want to go on that trip! His uneasiness about the trip said it all!" And here is a significant reason for listening to *"the inward witness."*

### TESTING THE INWARD WITNESS

Sometimes you might want to test the *'inward witness.'* That is how you will know whether it is your flesh leading you or not. For instance, when your wife asks you to visit your in-laws, you might hesitate to do so because you know within you that that is one place you have stopped going because of the issues they bring up. When you finally decide to speak to God about this, and you ask, "God is it truly you?" you are not asking the right question.

What you should ask instead, to test if it is your flesh speaking or not, is, "Does my flesh love going to see my in-laws?" There you have it! Your flesh will not tell you to go and see your in-laws based on your disposition towards going there. So, it cannot be your flesh leading you in this instance because it never likes going to the in-laws anyway. At this point, it should become clear that God is the One giving you the green light to visit your in-laws.

Paul said, *"I perceive"*; this is the first significant way God leads you, through *"the inward witness."* It is a go-ahead or green light.

There is a restaurant I frequented when I was in Port Harcourt back then. At that time, my wife had not yet moved to Port Harcourt. Whenever I was hungry, I would rush there to eat—I loved their food so much. Then one day, as I got into the car, as usual, to dash down there, the

Holy Spirit told me that I should not go there! It was not a voice; it was the inward witness. As much as I loved their food and so badly wanted to go there, I knew deep down it was the "inward witness" giving me a red light. So, I turned around.

I was thinking that perhaps, the red light was going to be for that day only. So, I waited for one week and wanted to go again, and I received the same witness. That was how I stopped going to that restaurant altogether. I later discovered that the woman who ran the restaurant was into the occult. But to God, be the glory forever, she repented sometime later and gave her life to Jesus Christ.

The point here is that you have to train yourself as you begin to walk with God. Do not take these things for granted. There are times when God will speak to you clearly and audibly, but indeed most times, "the inward witness" is the way He will lead you.

I have changed jobs by the inward witness. The first job I changed was by the inward witness. I just started having this uneasy feeling about the job, and I began checking in my spirit to know if it was God's Spirit or my flesh. Each passing day, it became stronger, and I knew it was the Lord saying it was time to move.

## 2. THE INWARD VOICE

Your spirit has a voice—the '*still small voice*'; a very quiet voice. I call it the voice of your conscience. It is the voice that will tell you clearly but quietly, '*do not go*' or '*go*'. The problem with this medium is that when you ignore it, you will stop hearing through it! Let me explain why: if you make hot tea, some people can drink it at 97 degrees, some at 95 degrees, and some others at 90 degrees. The difference is that some people are used to drinking it very hot. That is why they can drink it hot, and others cannot consume it at that temperature. Those who no longer feel the hotness of tea are like those who are impervious to the Holy Spirit's voice via this medium—they are unable to respond because it is as though their conscience is seared as with a hot iron.

> "*Now the Spirit speaketh expressly, that in the latter times some shall depart from the faith, giving heed to seducing spirits, and doctrines of devils; [2]Speaking lies in hypocrisy; having their conscience seared with a hot iron;*" (**1 Timothy 4:1-2**)

As a way of bolstering the 'tea analogy', the above scripture says that at a particular point of resistance, the Holy Spirit will not speak again or worse still, you will not hear Him again. In other words, like the hot tea and the lips of those who no longer feel the heat, you may ultimately lose the ability to hear Him over time. How sad that is!

There was once a rumour about a girl who was having an affair with her boss. One day, God began to speak—by the *'still small voice'*—and said I should tell the girl to stop that activity. I tried to argue that I did not have proof and that it was all wild rumours. But the moment the still small voice spoke, I knew that if I did not respond promptly, I would develop resistance and will not hear again. So, I called her and told her what the Lord had asked me to say to her. Instantly, she broke down and began to weep profusely.

She confessed that she had been trying to end the affair but that it was her boss who gave her the job and would not let her be; otherwise, he would have her sacked, and she did not know what else to do. In the meantime, I was excited inside me, thanking God that she did not take offence with my message and punch me in the face! Long story short, God ended the affair with her cooperation, of course, and she still kept her job! Glory to God!

The take away from this experience is that you need to consciously develop yourself to be sensitive to the Holy Spirit's prodding; otherwise, you might not hear Him. There is too much 'noise' around that can distract you. But you can sharpen your receptivity and focus your attention on hearing the *'still small voice.'* How can one achieve this?

> *"I say the truth in Christ, I lie not, my conscience also bearing me witness in the Holy Ghost." (**Romans 9:1**)*

Note that Paul said, *"my conscience bearing me witness."* That is a key phrase. It means that when God spoke to Paul through his spirit, he complied with whatever God said. Hence, he wrote, *"I follow my conscience"*—that *'still small voice'*.

> *"And Paul, earnestly beholding the council, said, Men and brethren, I have lived in all good conscience before God until this day." (**Acts 23:1**)*

Paul was drawing the attention of the Council to the fact that he always obeyed his conscience. If you do not follow the *'still small voice'*, you will lose the privilege of hearing God speak. I pray that the Lord will help you always to listen and obey the *'still small voice'* because it is a critical element in hearing from the Good Shepherd.

## 3. THE VOICE OF THE HOLY SPIRIT

You cannot miss the Holy Spirit's voice when He speaks because it is authoritative. In **1 Samuel 3**, when God was calling Samuel, that was the voice of the Holy Spirit! He can speak to you directly or via the still small voice, but it is always authoritative! Sometimes, it is almost quite audible. I remember once that I was on my knees praying in a guest house in Lagos. As I was praying, I heard, "Beware of almighty June!" I turned around, and there was nobody there. It was the Holy Spirit!

Now, the phrase "almighty June" meant "examination" to me. While at university, there were the end-of-session examinations and end-of-semester examinations. The end-of-session examinations usually took place in June—hence, "almighty June"—which symbolized a tough or big examination, as the end-of-semester examinations involved less voluminous reading!

Based on that understanding, the message meant that I was to prepare for an upcoming examination—a trial, a test, a temptation—that I must pass! Then I prayed to God that in the coming ordeal, He would help me to overcome. In June of that year, while watching the television, a news item stated that the government had ordered all the expatriates in the company I was working for to leave the country within twenty-four hours!

Some months after that, I got a call from the company's Human Resource Manager (HRM), who said that he wanted to speak to me about my career. I met with him, and he informed me that another multinational company called to say that they wanted to hire me. My employer's issues were still unresolved, but here I was with the HRM, who was informing me of another company that wanted to hire me—I had not written any application or consulted with anyone.

When I got to the multinational company that requested to hire me, they asked me to introduce myself, so I told them my name and said that I am born-again by God's grace. The woman in charge smiled at my introduction. I wanted to know who told them about me, but she smiled and said she wanted to hire me. She then arranged an interview for me, at the end of which all seven members on the panel wanted me to work for their department.

Why was all of that happening? It was because I had heard from God and prayed appropriately. When you hear His voice, you can never go wrong! It might look as if there is no way, but there will always be a way with Him—once you hear His voice!

I recall an experience back then while working in the Niger Delta. There was this day I wanted to go to Port Harcourt to see my fiancée (now my wife). Then I heard, "Don't go to Port Harcourt!"; I looked around to be sure nobody was around. At that stage in my life, I was quite stubborn, so I began questioning who spoke to me when that voice came. At the time, I did not see any reason why I should not make the trip. So, I jumped into the car and left for Port Harcourt. When I got to Port Harcourt, I learnt that my fiancée had left for my station that morning, meaning that I had missed her on the way! It then became clear why God wanted to save me the trouble of going to Port Harcourt, knowing that she was coming to meet me. That was why He said, "Don't go!"

Until that day, my fiancée had never been to my station, so I did not think she could come there, but God knew all along. With Him, it is never about a pattern. Although she had never been there before on her own, God knew she was on her way. It is possibly why many car crashes have happened in the past because the culprits did not listen to the Holy Spirit's voice when forwarned not to embark on some trips! That is how also, many times, we blame God when things go wrong, forgetting that He has put things in place to guide and lead us in all situations! Thankfully, God did not let me end up in a car accident on that occasion!

#### 4. DREAMS

The easy one for many is when God speaks to them through a dream, and it is very straightforward. Everyone likes that because there will be no problem understanding it all at once. Through dreams, God gives us instructions, warnings, etc.

I once worked for a company, and there was a Boardroom power tussle. Some Executive Directors (EDs) wanted to unseat the Chairman. I sided with the EDs. After a meeting with the EDs on a strategy against the

Chairman, I had a dream the same night.

In the dream, God said to me, "Why are you fighting the Chairman? Why are you teaming up with the EDs against the Chairman?" He asked if I would join the EDs in their lawsuit against the Chairman, and I said, "No." He queried how I could be involved in all that and still claim to be praying for the Chairman. At that point, I woke up, went on my knees to pray. At that moment, my phone rang; lo and behold, it was the Chairman calling me from overseas. He informed me the EDs were threatening to take over his company and that the matter was now in court.

In the morning, I called one of the EDs and told him that I was no longer on their side in the matter! He wanted to know why, and I told him what God said to me about them taking the Chairman to court, but he denied it! But God cannot lie! Indeed, the EDs had gone to court, accusing the Chairman of inability to continue as Chairman of the Board. Thankfully, I had nothing to do with it anymore because God had forwarned me through a dream! God still speaks to His sheep through dreams!

Sometimes, a dream might need interpretation because the message might not be clear to you. That is when you need the guidance of the Holy Spirit. Differentiating the Old Testament Dispensation from the New Testament Dispensation is that divine messages during the former were mostly through the prophets, but in the latter, they come directly to all believers. Therefore, any revelation from a secondary source should be a confirmation of what the Holy Spirit has told you. Also, note that no revelation from God can contradict the written word of God!

*God still speaks to His sheep through dreams!*

### 5. IN A VISION

A vision comes in two ways: An open vision or a closed vision.

Saul was led by an open vision in **Acts 9** when God intercepted him at Damascus Road. Similarly, when God told Mary about the birth of Jesus Christ, He appeared to her in an open vision. She was not asleep.

> *"And in the sixth month the angel Gabriel was sent from God unto a city of Galilee, named Nazareth, [27]To a virgin espoused to a man whose name was Joseph, of the house of*

*David; and the virgin's name was Mary. ²⁸And the angel came in unto her, and said, Hail, thou that art highly favoured, the Lord is with thee: blessed art thou among women. ²⁹And when she saw him, she was troubled at his saying, and cast in her mind what manner of salutation this should be. ³⁰And the angel said unto her, Fear not, Mary: for thou hast found favour with God." (**Luke 1:26-30**)*

When God spoke with Gideon in the winepress when he was hiding from the Midianites, it was an open vision.

*"And there came an angel of the LORD, and sat under an oak which was in Ophrah, that pertained unto Joash the Abi–ezrite: and his son Gideon threshed wheat by the winepress, to hide it from the Midianites. ¹²And the angel of the LORD appeared unto him, and said unto him, The LORD is with thee, thou mighty man of valour. ¹³And Gideon said unto him, Oh my Lord, if the LORD be with us, why then is all this befallen us? and where be all his miracles which our fathers told us of, saying, Did not the LORD bring us up from Egypt? but now the LORD hath forsaken us, and delivered us into the hands of the Midianites. ¹⁴And the LORD looked upon him, and said, Go in this thy might, and thou shalt save Israel from the hand of the Midianites: have not I sent thee? ¹⁵And he said unto him, Oh my Lord, wherewith shall I save Israel? behold, my family is poor in Manasseh, and I am the least in my father's house. ¹⁶And the LORD said unto him, Surely I will be with thee, and thou shalt smite the Midianites as one man. ¹⁷And he said unto him, If now I have found grace in thy sight, then shew me a sign that thou talkest with me. ¹⁸Depart not hence, I pray thee, until I come unto thee, and bring forth my present, and set it before thee. And he said, I will tarry until thou come again. ¹⁹And Gideon went in, and made ready a kid, and unleavened cakes of an ephah of flour: the flesh he put in a basket, and he put the broth in a pot, and brought it out unto him under the oak, and presented it. ²⁰And the angel of God said unto him, Take the flesh and the unleavened cakes, and lay them upon this rock, and pour out the broth. And he did so. ²¹Then the angel of the LORD put forth the end of the staff that was in his hand, and touched*

> *the flesh and the unleavened cakes; and there rose up fire out of the rock, and consumed the flesh and the unleavened cakes. Then the angel of the LORD departed out of his sight.* *²²And when Gideon perceived that he was an angel of the LORD, Gideon said, Alas, O Lord GOD! for because I have seen an angel of the LORD face to face. ²³And the LORD said unto him, Peace be unto thee; fear not: thou shalt not die. ²⁴Then Gideon built an altar there unto the LORD, and called it Jehovah–shalom: unto this day it is yet in Ophrah of the Abi–ezrites." (**Judges 6:11-24**)*

He appeared to Cornelius, a Gentile, in an open vision.

> *"There was a certain man in Cæsarea called Cornelius, a centurion of the band called the Italian band, ²A devout man, and one that feared God with all his house, which gave much alms to the people, and prayed to God alway. ³He saw in a vision evidently about the ninth hour of the day an angel of God coming in to him, and saying unto him, Cornelius. ⁴And when he looked on him, he was afraid, and said, What is it, Lord? And he said unto him, Thy prayers and thine alms are come up for a memorial before God." (**Acts 10:1-4**)*

With Ananias, it was also an open vision. God knew Ananias very well. How could He tell him to go and pray for Saul, a man who was notorious for persecuting and killing believers? The man would just run away. That is why He needed to reach him via an open vision.

> *"And there was a certain disciple at Damascus, named Ananias; and to him said the Lord in a vision, Ananias. And he said, Behold, I am here, Lord. ¹¹And the Lord said unto him, Arise, and go into the street which is called Straight, and enquire in the house of Judas for one called Saul, of Tarsus: for, behold, he prayeth." (**Acts 9:10-11**)*

The truth is, when you read the Bible, you will discover that the people whom God led through open vision are relatively few. Though there are still people led by open visions today, such occurrences are not very common. Once in a while, we hear of people who experienced angelic visitation. I doubt if you have seen one yourself. I have not seen one myself, but I recall that I was moved by the Holy Ghost once during a service to declare that some of those present would have an angelic visitation. Within a week, a sister came to testify that an angel had visited her.

A closed vision, on the other hand, is when God speaks to you in a trance. The distinction here is that you are not awake, but you are also not sound asleep. An example is when God spoke to Peter while on Simon's housetop (the tanner).

> *On the morrow, as they went on their journey, and drew nigh unto the city, Peter went up upon the housetop to pray about the sixth hour:* [10]*And he became very hungry, and would have eaten: but while they made ready, he fell into a trance,* [11]*And saw heaven opened, and a certain vessel descending unto him, as it had been a great sheet knit at the four corners, and let down to the earth:* [12]*Wherein were all manner of fourfooted beasts of the earth, and wild beasts, and creeping things, and fowls of the air.* [13]*And there came a voice to him, Rise, Peter; kill, and eat.* [14]*But Peter said, Not so, Lord; for I have never eaten any thing that is common or unclean.* [15]*And the voice spake unto him again the second time, What God hath cleansed, that call not thou common.* [16]*This was done thrice: and the vessel was received up again into heaven. (Acts 10:9-16)*

*Every communication received through visions must be scriptural and consistent with God's nature!*

God used this incident to prepare Peter for the visit of Cornelius' people who came to fetch him so they could hear the gospel — the first time the Gentiles were to listen to the gospel!

It is crucial to know that every communication received through visions must be scriptural and consistent with God's nature! For example, if you have problems with your wife, and an 'angel' appears to you and asks you to go and marry another wife, you will have to show us in the Bible where such is permitted! You will have to prove it through the authority of Scripture! If there is no scriptural precedence to support your 'vision', then clearly, God did not speak to you; the devil did! And in the case of divorce and remarriage, there is no scriptural support for it!

*"Prove all things; hold fast that which is good."* (**1 Thessalonians 5:21**)

The above scripture text is the standard!

## 6. MEDITATION ON SCRIPTURE

When you read the Bible and meditate on God's word, God can minister to you through the *inward witness*, using *scripture, the voice of the Spirit* or the *still small voice* backed up by Scripture. Someone can be ministering or preaching to you, and from what he is saying, you can hear the voice of God as they minister.

## 7. WORD OF KNOWLEDGE

A word of knowledge comes from God when He provides insight into a situation you may be going through. He may give you the information directly or through someone else. It can happen during the teaching or preaching of God's word, exhortation or any other time as led by the Holy Spirit. Many people who have been to the Redemption Camp would have experienced that while Pastor Adeboye is ministering, God would most times reveal something about someone in the congregation to him. He would typically begin by saying, "There is someone here, the Lord says…" This is a word of knowledge.

I was in Port Harcourt one time, and there was this day when someone came to wrestle with me all night. Even though it was a spiritual battle, I could see that the attacker was a physical being. We fought for a long time. I knew he was not an angel of God, nor was he sent by God; I could see that this was a demonic being. By the morning, I was tired because of the intensity of the fight. "Who are these people that will not even let someone have a good sleep?" I had wondered out loud after the experience. And it happened that that day was a Friday, so I went to Redemption Camp. When I got there, Pastor Adeboye had barely preached for ten minutes before a word came, and He said, "The Lord says there is someone here; those who came to fight you all night long are all dead!" I knew that was for me, and I shouted, "Amen!" After that day, they never showed up again! I knew God was speaking to me at the camp meeting that day, and it came via the word of knowledge.

# HOW TO TRAIN YOUR SPIRIT

As with all spiritual things, we need to train our spirit to respond appropriately to the Spirit of God. Do not forget that your spirit had been dormant—dead—for so long, and you have been listening to other voices—your feelings, your reasoning, rationalization, what you see with your eyes, etc. So, how do you train your spirit?

## 1. MEDITATE ON THE WORD

To meditate on the word of God is to ponder it or ruminate over it, and it can involve reciting scripture verses and allowing the Holy Spirit to explain what the verses mean and the implication for you.

> *"This book of the law shall not depart out of thy mouth; but thou shalt meditate therein day and night, that thou mayest observe to do according to all that is written therein: for then thou shalt make thy way prosperous, and then thou shalt have good success." (**Joshua 1:8**)*

> *"Blessed is the man that walketh not in the counsel of the ungodly, nor standeth in the way of sinners, nor sitteth in the seat of the scornful. ²But his delight is in the law of the LORD; and in his law doth he meditate day and night." (**Psalm 1:1-2**)*

## 2. PRACTICE THE WORD

When you read the Bible or when God speaks a word to you, you must act on the word as it ministers to you. If you hear the word of God and do not put it to practise or apply what you have read or heard, you will be one of those the Bible describes as forgetful hearers!

> *But be ye doers of the word, and not hearers only, deceiving your own selves. ²³For if any be a hearer of the word, and not a doer, he is like unto a man beholding his natural face in a glass: ²⁴For he beholdeth himself, and goeth his way, and straightway forgetteth what manner of man he was. ²⁵But whoso looketh into the perfect law of liberty, and continueth therein, he being not a forgetful hearer, but a doer*

*of the work, this man shall be blessed in his deed. (**James 1:22-25**)*

As you put to practice the word of God, you become more assertive in the faith—remember that

*faith cometh by hearing, and hearing by the word of God (**Romans 10:17**)*

Also, the word of God builds or illuminates us in the faith and our relationship with the Good Shepherd and helps us to appreciate what He is instructing us to do practically.

*"But ye, beloved, building up yourselves on your most holy faith, praying in the Holy Ghost," (**Jude 1:20**)*

*"And now, brethren, I commend you to God, and to the word of his grace, which is able to build you up, and to give you an inheritance among all them which are sanctified." (**Acts 20:32**)*

### 3. GIVE THE WORD FIRST PLACE

*Thus saith the LORD, The heaven is my throne, and the earth is my footstool: where is the house that ye build unto me? and where is the place of my rest? ²For all those things hath mine hand made, and all those things have been, saith the LORD: but to this man will I look, even to him that is poor and of a contrite spirit, and trembleth at my word. (**Isaiah 66:1-2**)*

We must prioritize acting on the word of God above everything else! Once God speaks to you about something, you have to do it immediately! Those who tremble at the word of God do not delay to carry out His instructions.

### 4. INSTANTLY OBEY THE VOICE OF YOUR SPIRIT

Delays create room for doubt and can easily make you develop resistance, ultimately silencing that channel. The truth is, you need all your hearing channels to hear God. And once you have heard the voice of God, do not hesitate to carry out His instruction.

## 5. ALWAYS PRAY IN TONGUES

> *"Likewise the Spirit also helpeth our infirmities: for we know not what we should pray for as we ought: but the Spirit itself maketh intercession for us with groanings which cannot be uttered."* (**Romans 8:26**)

When you pray in tongues, the Spirit prays! You are more sensitive at that point. I have come to know in my walk with God that, many times, when He speaks to me, and I begin to speak in tongues, the message becomes more explicit. When there is an inward witness, and I start to pray in tongues, it becomes clearer.

*Sometimes, God presents you with several options but wants you to come to Him before choosing one!*

When "the still small voice" speaks to you and you begin to pray in tongues, it becomes more evident. And if it is "the authoritative voice of God", you cannot miss that! You could be looking around for someone, like my driver's experience the day God spoke to him in Port Harcourt. He usually would go to see native doctors, then one day, God spoke to him. He was getting ready to consult a native doctor when he heard, very loudly and clearly, "You! Can I not help you? Why do you go every day to see native doctors?" Startled, the man started looking around his bedroom to see if there was someone else there with him! That was the day his life changed!

## 6. PRACTICE GOING TO GOD IN PRAYER ON EVERY MATTER

I desire that as you grow in your walk with God, that you will get to that point where you can authoritatively say, "The Lord told me….!" That is the ultimate level in following the Good Shepherd!

What happens when you have to decide on more than one option? What do you do when there is more than one alternative to the result? If you have not been practising praying to God on every matter, no matter how seemingly insignificant, you will end up choosing by sight, feeling, thought, etc.

For example, if the Lord allows you to receive two or more job offers, which would you choose? What would you do to know which one to choose? The answer lies in prayer. In deciding which job to pick, you must ask God, and He will speak to you.

Sometimes, God presents you with several options to show you that He can give you anything, but He still wants you to come to Him before choosing one, as a sign of your total dependence on Him. Sometimes, God can allow many suitors to approach a lady to see what she would do. Would she go to God for counsel or be tempted to make her own choice? Would she consider the one who looks *'together'*—tall, handsome, and seemingly has everything? Does she know if the 'together' suitor borrowed the car he went to see her with? Indeed, the suitor who has nothing now may have a far better prospect and depth than the 'together' guy! Only God knows!

So, when *the inward witness* gives the green light for that seemingly broke brother because God sees many things the sister cannot see, she may begin to draw God's attention to the state of the guy's shoes! Thus, the Bible says, *Let God lead you!*

*"For we walk by faith, not by sight"* (**2 Corinthians 5:7**)

# TO KNOW GOD AND TO BE LED BY HIM IS THE ULTIMATE!

By now, we should no longer be querying God when things happen because now you know that He loves you, died on the cross to prove it, and has given you all things that pertain to life and godliness. And just in case anyone is trying hard to provide you with a false sense of fulfilment elsewhere, God says that His plans for you are far better!

> *"For I know the thoughts that I think toward you, saith the LORD, thoughts of peace, and not of evil, to give you an expected end"* (**Jeremiah 29:11**)

He is the Good Shepherd, the One who will never fail you. That much I can attest to, from walking with Him.

Let God lead you!

# PART THREE

## *The Good Shepherd Leadership Model (TGSLM)*

# TABLE OF CONTENTS FOR PART THREE

# Chapter 9

**The Good Shepherd**

# A New Leadership Paradigm

*Oh! to be like Thee, full of compassion,*

*Loving, forgiving, tender and kind,*

*Helping the helpless, cheering the fainting,*

*Seeking the wand'ring sinner to find*

*Stanza 2 of "Oh! to be Like Thee" (1897)*
*by Thomas Obediah Chisholm, 1866-1960*

*'Verily, verily, I say unto you, He that entereth not by the door into the sheepfold, but climbeth up some other way, the same is a thief and a robber. ²But he that entereth in by the door is the shepherd of the sheep. ³To him the porter openeth; and the sheep hear his voice: and he calleth his own sheep by name, and leadeth them out. ⁴And when he putteth forth his own sheep, he goeth before them, and the sheep follow him: for they know his voice. ⁵And a stranger will they not follow, but will flee from him: for they know not the voice of strangers.' ⁶This parable spake Jesus unto them: but they understood not what things they were which he spake unto them. ⁷Then said Jesus unto them again, 'Verily, verily, I say unto you, I am the door of the sheep. ⁸All that ever came before me are thieves and robbers: but the sheep did not hear them. ⁹I am the door: by me if any man enter in, he shall be saved, and shall go in and out, and find pasture. ¹⁰The thief cometh not, but for to steal, and to kill, and to destroy: I am come that they might have life, and that they might have it more abundantly. ¹¹I am the good shepherd: the good shepherd giveth his life for the sheep. ¹²But he that is an hireling, and not the shepherd, whose own the sheep are not, seeth the wolf coming, and leaveth the sheep, and fleeth: and the wolf catcheth them, and scattereth the sheep. ¹³The hireling fleeth, because he is an hireling, and careth not for the sheep. ¹⁴I am the good shepherd, and know my sheep, and am known of mine. ¹⁵As the Father knoweth me, even so know I the Father: and I lay down my life for the sheep."* **(John 10:1-15)**

L et us examine the above scripture text, which has been the primary text for this book, to lay the groundwork for our discussion in this chapter. Understanding is the key driver for change, but when the Lord spoke this parable to them, they did not understand it.

*This parable spake Jesus unto them: but they understood not what things they were which he spake unto them.* **(John 10:6)**

Understanding is the key to getting the flow of **John 10** in the context of our discussion on *A New Leadership Paradigm*. It is evident that, like many of His allegories, the import of this parable was lost on many when He spoke it and is still so for several people today—Christians and non-Christians alike. But unknown to many is that in this parable lies the ultimate leadership blueprint for all time.

By God's grace and Spirit who inspires understanding, we shall show the biblical model for authentic leadership that has been hiding in plain sight for ages, even to this time. The Bible says:

> *"Wisdom is the principal thing; therefore, get wisdom: and with all thy getting get understanding." (**Proverbs 4:7**)*

May God grant us wisdom and understanding to appreciate and appropriate the authentic leadership model in our affairs as Christians—be they secular or spiritual. So what is the pathway of authentic leadership through the golden standard of God's word?

# A NEW ORDER

Before Jesus came on to the scene, the Roman Empire had conquered the world, and they ruled based on the Greek leadership model. Under this model, a leader is a *Master*—one who is feared and served at all times. But Christ came on the scene with a significant disruption as He upended that model. He struck at the heart of the Roman and Greek authoritarian leadership model when He began to teach the tenets of *Servant-Leadership*!

Throughout one evening's teaching, Jesus taught His disciples to desire servanthood as the basis for greatness! He said if you want to lead a group, you must become the servant of that group—it may be a company, a ministry, an organization, a home, a cooperative, etc.! That was new and strange to their ears. He drew a sharp contrast with the world's system, pointing out how the Gentiles lord it over their subjects. Let us hear from the Master through **The Message** translation of Scripture:

> *"It was about that time that the mother of the Zebedee brothers came with her two sons and knelt before Jesus with a request. [21]"What do you want?" Jesus asked. She said, "Give your word that these two sons of mine will be award-*

*ed the highest places of honor in your kingdom, one at your right hand, one at your left hand." ²²Jesus responded, "You have no idea what you're asking." And he said to James and John, "Are you capable of drinking the cup that I'm about to drink?" They said, "Sure, why not?" ²³Jesus said, "Come to think of it, you are going to drink my cup. But as to awarding places of honor, that's not my business. My Father is taking care of that." ²⁴⁻²⁸When the ten others heard about this, they lost their tempers, thoroughly disgusted with the two brothers. So Jesus got them together to settle things down. He said, "You've observed how godless rulers throw their weight around, how quickly a little power goes to their heads. It's not going to be that way with you. Whoever wants to be great must become a servant. Whoever wants to be first among you must be your slave. That is what the Son of Man has done: He came to serve, not be served—and then to give away his life in exchange for the many who are held hostage." (**Matthew 20:20-28, MSG**)*

Jesus said that the leader must be ready to serve rather than be served. And the most significant part of Christ's leadership style is that He gave His life for His sheep. That is the highest point of service! It is contrary to what obtains in the world's system. There, leaders are protected at all cost by their subjects.

Jesus' leadership model thus represents a massive break from the norm. This model pivots on an overriding love for others! It is the core message of all of Jesus' teachings and life's work!

## THE FOUR ELEMENTS OF THE GOOD SHEPHERD LEADERSHIP MODEL (TGSLM)

It is pertinent to state that the four elements we are about to examine are extensions of the core essentials of Christ's leadership qualities which we discussed in Part One of this book. The Lord Jesus is qualified to lead His sheep because He knows the terrain, the way—the way of eternal life, of salvation, and of prosperity and abundance—,the right step to take in every situation, and what you are going through.

God-inspired leadership is the sum of the four elements that are enumerated below. These elements are wrapped about the Good Shepherd's attributes, which we discussed in Part One of this book. These qualities encapsulate what Jesus's leadership model is all about. The attributes of the Good Shepherd distinguish Him from secular parallels. For easier comprehension, we have tried to represent these winning ways in our everyday conventional terms.

These four God-inspired leadership model elements are; having a connection to an authentic authority, emotional intelligence inspired by divine guidance, a servant-first-before-leader paradigm, and compassionate leadership. Let us look at them in some detail.

## 1—CONNECTION TO AUTHENTIC AUTHORITY

**John 10:1-15** makes it evident that as the Good Shepherd, Jesus operates from a realm of valid or authentic authority. He calls the sheep His own; the potter knows Him to be genuine; His Father sent Him. Everything about Him is legitimate—backed by the Father's authority! For these reasons, the sheep love and align with Him.

In the secular parallel, you will find that many who claim to be leaders are not qualified to be called by that title at all. Too many came in through the window. Their tenure in the organization they oversee is fraught with challenges, including staff disloyalty, under-capacity, and poor service delivery. But the Good Shepherd is 100% legit! The Good Shepherd's approach is the way to win with people and with God.

Fortunately, you can achieve legitimacy to become a better leader today by aligning with God's authority. It begins with accepting Jesus Christ as your Lord and personal Saviour. Then, it will become easier to make other things right. When Jesus is your authority, you have authentic authority because He delegates His authority to you—but remember that that authority is for service, not to bear rule!

## 2—EMOTIONAL INTELLIGENCE INSPIRED BY DIVINE GUIDANCE

Beyond the impact of works such as Daniel Goleman's *"Emotional Intelligence"*, the field of emotional intelligence has assumed greater importance in today's workplace. The ability to manage people and their emotional state to achieve optimal performance on the job is one big headache for today's managers at all levels. Many times, this is the difference between high and low performing teams. While many are pursuing improvements in this regard, many more do not know what to do.

The good news is that the Good Shepherd always has the best solution to every problem.

> *"Therefore, all things whatsoever ye would that men should do to you, do ye even so to them: for this is the law and the prophets." (**Matthew 7:12-13**)*

Also known as *the Golden Rule,* this scriptural precept is the antidote to all conflict-infested teams if properly applied, especially in tandem with the gift of wisdom which the Good Shepherd has in abundance and gives freely to all who desire it.

> *"If any of you lack wisdom, let him ask of God, that giveth to all men liberally, and upbraideth not; and it shall be given him." (**James 1:5**)*

*Serving the led is the crux of Jesus' teaching on the subject of leadership.*

### 3 — SERVANT-FIRST-BEFORE-A-LEADER IDEOLOGY

> *"But Jesus called them unto him, and said, "Ye know that the princes of the Gentiles exercise dominion over them, and they that are great exercise authority upon them. [26]But it shall not be so among you: but whosoever will be great among you, let him be your minister; [27]And whosoever will be chief among you, let him be your servant: [28]Even as the Son of man came not to be ministered unto, but to minister, and to give his life a ransom for many." (**Matthew 20:25-28**)*

In TGSLM, a leader is first the servant of the led. Now, this is not some pretentious attempt to look good in the public eye; instead, it is *serving* the people you are leading!

Serving the led is the crux of Jesus' teaching on the subject of leadership. The Good Shepherd was the first partaker of His teaching as he drove home the message of serving the led by washing His disciple's feet! Let us examine this:

> *"Now before the feast of the passover, when Jesus knew that his hour was come that he should depart out of this world unto the Father, having loved his own which were in the world, he loved them unto the end. ²And supper being ended, the devil having now put into the heart of Judas Iscariot, Simon's son, to betray him; ³Jesus knowing that the Father had given all things into his hands, and that he was come from God, and went to God; ⁴He riseth from supper, and laid aside his garments; and took a towel, and girded himself. ⁵After that he poureth water into a bason, and began to wash the disciples' feet, and to wipe them with the towel wherewith he was girded. ⁶Then cometh he to Simon Peter: and Peter saith unto him, Lord, dost thou wash my feet? ⁷Jesus answered and said unto him, What I do thou knowest not now; but thou shalt know hereafter. ⁸Peter saith unto him, Thou shalt never wash my feet. Jesus answered him, If I wash thee not, thou hast no part with me. ⁹Simon Peter saith unto him, Lord, not my feet only, but also my hands and my head. ¹⁰Jesus saith to him, He that is washed needeth not save to wash his feet, but is clean every whit: and ye are clean, but not all. ¹¹For he knew who should betray him; therefore said he, Ye are not all clean. ¹²So after he had washed their feet, and had taken his garments, and was set down again, he said unto them, Know ye what I have done to you? ¹³Ye call me Master and Lord: and ye say well; for so I am." ¹⁴If I then, your Lord and Master, have washed your feet; ye also ought to wash one another's feet. ¹⁵For I have given you an example, that ye should do as I have done to you. (**John 13:1-15**)*

Let us break it down some more. Jesus is not your everyday '*bossy boss*' leader. That is what obtains in the World System, where positions intoxicate those who hold them. While Jesus' model does not despise rank and file, it also has no place for the pride that comes with it! Think about it: if, as a manager, you had to wash your subordinates' feet monthly, can you imagine what kind of connection you would have with them? It most certainly cannot be a "bossy boss" connection; rather, it will be that of "*a caring mother!*" Think deeply about it! Caring and consideration for others is what TGSLM entails! Whether it is with subordinates, customers, or citizens.

## 4—COMPASSIONATE LEADERSHIP

>"⁴And when he putteth forth his own sheep, he goeth before them, and the sheep follow him: for they know his voice.
>
>¹¹I am the good shepherd: the good shepherd giveth his life for the sheep.
>
>²⁸And I give unto them eternal life; and they shall never perish, neither shall any man pluck them out of my hand. ²⁹My Father, which gave them me, is greater than all; and no man is able to pluck them out of my Father's hand."(*John 10: 4, 11, 28-29*)

It is instructive to note that the leadership equation he presents in this parable is the relationship between a shepherd and his sheep. This relationship, especially from the shepherd's angle, is inspired by the divine perspective of agape love—having a genuine interest in, and passion for, the sheep—and these may be subordinates, customers, clients, citizens.

A shepherd cares about his sheep profoundly and is always willing to protect and nurture them regardless of the cost—even if that means paying the ultimate price for them! And Jesus did pay the maximum price through His sacrificial death on the cross to redeem all of humanity. What a Leader He is!

*Authentic leadership cannot be that of a "bossy boss"; rather, it will be that of "a caring mother!"*

Notable in Jesus' approach is that He first rescues the lost before dealing with their sin-problem. He does not 'rub' their sins on their faces and flog them with the weight of their guilt. No! Instead, he would save them from their troubles, solve their problems, and offer salvation as a pathway to eternal life and victorious living, henceforth. This pattern of leadership is consistent in all the miracles Jesus performed during His earthly ministry.

Now, that is the kind of leadership quality today's workplace has been struggling to replicate, with very little success. While human wisdom has made people commit millions of dollars in training, workshops, and seminars to acquire this highly desirable leadership skill, God's people have an invaluable resource in the Bible for tapping into such!

What is more, by following the Good Shepherd, you have access to being led in the *'Alpha and Omega dimension'*: this is a vantage point of knowing God's voice and hearing 'the One Who knows the beginning through to the ending' of any matter, speak to you! You could call it *'the unfair advantage'* because you now have 'access to divine information in a competitive business space!' To operate in this realm is dependent on the depth of your knowledge of Him.

# FINAL WORDS

*"But grow in grace, and in the knowledge of our Lord and Saviour Jesus Christ. To him be glory both now and forever." (**2 Peter 3:18**)*

As we come to the close of this book, I pray that you have gained a deeper understanding of God's Character and ways. Equally important is that you comprehend what is required to walk with God and be led by Him.

*Seeing then that God's plan for your life is far better than any program you can come up with, what manner of Christian should you be?*

God's plan for you is far better than you can ever imagine—not in your wildest dreams! He reassures you to that effect when He says:

*"For I know the thoughts that I think toward you, saith the LORD, thoughts of peace, and not of evil, to give you an expected end." (**Jeremiah 29:11**)*

Because Jesus is the Good Shepherd, His thoughts for the sheep are always thoughts of peace and well-being!

*"I will instruct thee and teach thee in the way which thou shalt go: I will guide thee with mine eye." (**Psalm 32:8**)*

Seeing then that God's plan for your life is far better than any program you can come up with, what manner of Christian should you be? It merely means that you must learn to have implicit faith in God! Gladly, this book has shown you the steps and processes that you need to follow to possess the ability to know and hear His voice.

*"Beloved, I wish above everything that thou mayest prosper and be in good health, even as thy soul prospereth." (**3 John 1:3**)*

Like John, the Beloved, prayed, your soul's prosperity is the ultimate goal of this book. And that is a function of how much you understand and connect with the Good Shepherd's leadership.

Life eternal, which is abundant life, is tied to knowing and following

Jesus! Nothing else will do! May testimonies abound in your life due to knowing and following the Good Shepherd, as sheep follow their shepherd!

# REFERENCES

1.   Hagin Kenneth E., *How You Can Be Led By The Spirit of God*, Second Edition, Tulsa Oklahoma, 1989, Kenneth Hagin Ministries.

2.   https://technext.ng/2019/08/02/streettech-pure-water-production-and-nafdac-how-safe-do-you-think-your-water-is/

Made in the USA
Monee, IL
26 June 2021

72342134R00098